PIONEER

A Pembrokeshire Pioneer

Bill Frost of Saundersfoot,
the first man to fly.

Roscoe Howells

© Text: Roscoe Howells

ISBN: 1-84524-084-7
978-1-84524-084-4

Cover design: Sian Parri

Published in July 2007
Llygad Gwalch, Ysgubor Plas, Llwyndyrys,
Pwllheli, Gwynedd LL53 6NG
☏ 01758 750432   🖷 01758 750438
🖰 gai@llygadgwalch.com   Web site: www.carreg-gwalch.co.uk

To the memory of the late
Paddy Hands.

A lovely lady, who gave enthusiastic and cheerful
help with so much vital research exploring various
records stored away in far distant London, and to
her husband John for his never failing support.

Saundersfoot Man Who Built An Aeroplane 40 Years Ago

DEATH OF THE GRAND OLD MAN OF AVIATION IN WALES

REMARKABLE STORY OF WM. FROST'S EARLY EXPERIMENTS

A career crowded with interest and ambition has been brought to a close by the death, which occurred on Friday last, of Mr. Wm. Frost, of St. Bride's Lane, Saundersfoot.

Mr. Frost, who was 87 years of age, had spent the greater part of his life in his native Saundersfoot, and he could claim to have been one of the pioneers of aircraft design. Half a century ago he was convinced that air transport was a practical proposition, and he designed, patented and built an aeroplane which was the first to be constructed in Britain.

At the time representatives from several foreign countries came to Saundersfoot to interview Mr. Frost and to endeavour to buy his patent. One offer, which was made by a German representative, would have made him a wealthy man had he accepted it, but he turned them all down in the hope that one day, when the plane was perfected to his satisfaction, he could offer the patent to his own Government.

The story of his achievement has aroused national interest and it was told in an article written by Mr. H. G. Walters (now Editor of the "Weekly News") which appeared in the "Western Mail" in 1932. The article is re-produced hereunder.

Mr. Frost, who had been blind for many years, died at the home of his daughter at Penybank, Ammanford. His wife predeceased him about six months ago. In his early days he was a vocalist and musician of considerable ability and for many years he was the conductor of the Saundersfoot Male Voice Party, of which he was the founder. Under his leadership this party captured many notable choral victories on the eisteddfod platform in Pembrokeshire and Carmarthenshire, Mr. Frost's favourite test piece being "The Psalm of Life."

He was a son of the late Mr. John Frost, of Saundersfoot, who was a Guardsman during the French invasion of Fishguard.

Mr. Frost was a conscientious worker, both socially and religiously, and his influence in these spheres was a strong force in the neighbourhood. He was a life-long member of Bethany Chapel, Saundersfoot, where he was also a deacon.

Besides the daughter there are two sons surviving, Mr. Wilfred J. Frost, who lives at Saundersfoot, and Mr. Lawson Frost, who resides at Barry.

until it lifted the lad completely off his feet for a second or two. With that gust of wind was born the first dream of wings that would ride through the air.

It was some years later before Frost commenced to put his schemes to the test. The problem before him was twofold; to raise the machine off the ground, and then to induce its motion through the air. The machine, therefore, became something of a "cross" between the airship and the glider. Petrol engines were then unknown. Frost had built and patented his flying machine a dozen years before the late M. Alberto Santos-Dumont, the world-famous aeronautical inventor, achieved the first fluttering hopes from the ground in a power-driven machine in August, 1906, and fifteen years before an authentic flight in a man-carrying aeroplane equipped with an engine was made by Orville Wright at Dayton, Ohio.

ONE-MAN POWER.

According to the specifications of Frost's machine it consisted of two cigar-like chambers, one above the other, constructed of wirework and covered with light waterproof material. The upper chamber was filled with hydrogen gas sufficient to lift the machine without its pilot.

In the lower compartment the pilot was sealed, and it was in order to provide the extra lifting power to raise both machine and passenger that Frost adopted the gyroscope principle. Above the upper chamber was a propeller—or what the inventor described as a "vertical fan."

It was attached to a steel shaft running down through the gas-chamber to the pilot's compartment. Here it was operated by the pilot by means of a bevelled friction gearing device, so that the pilot was able to wind the propeller until it attained sufficient force to raise the machine into the air.

There were two wings, one on either side of the gas-chamber, and when a certain height had been attained the pilot would stop the hand-driven propeller. It was then that the gliding motion would become effective. The machine would travel downwards and onwards until momentum had been gained. It was directed upwards again by a tail rudder worked by wires from the pilot's compartment, the upward gradients being also aided by the hand-driven propeller. While the tail rudder directed the upward and downward motion, a similar device on the front of the machine controlled its sideways direction.

Just as the gyroscope propeller served to raise the craft, so it enabled the pilot to regulate a gentle landing.

Contents

Foreword 10
Chapter 1
    The First Flight 11
Chapter 2
    The Storm 14
Chapter 3
    The Quest of Icarus 19
Chapter 4
    Who Was Bill Frost? 24
Chapter 5
    How It Began 34
Chapter 6
    Our Fathers Have Told Us 42
Chapter 7
    What The Papers Said 68
Chapter 8
    Bill Frost's Flying Machine 82
Chapter 9
    The Years of Disillusionment 88
Chapter 10
    What Happened To the Papers
    and Why The Long Silence? 95
Chapter 11
    Why The Sudden Interest? 103
Chapter 12
    After Jeff Bellingham 109

Acknowledgements

As has been said so often, one of the most difficult tasks when writing a book, and especially one involving so much research, is knowing who and how many to thank once it is finished.

Having heard the oft told story of Bill Frost, been so close to it and to so many who knew so much of the facts, talked about and heard it talked about at odd times, for more than eighty years, I have never ever had the slightest doubt that he did indeed fly. So perhaps I should thank first of all those who have urged me to write of the facts as I know them so that the world can give a good man his due.

So many people are mentioned in the text that my indebtedness to them will be self-evident and, rather than refer to them all by name here, I hope they will accept this as an expression of my appreciation. There is one not referred to by name, and to her the book is dedicated. My thanks, too, to one more not named in the text, Donald Johns, village native and long-time friend, for his generous Foreword.

The many who have helped, however, but are named only in the text will perhaps forgive me if I do indeed mention just the one by name here, and that is Jeff Bellingham, who came here all the way from Minnesota to ensure that the great story was not allowed to die unrecorded.

As ever, without exception, or mentioning individuals by name, there has been the never failing help, courtesy and friendship of the staff at the Pembrokeshire County Records Office, as well as, on the odd occasion when necessary, at the Pembrokeshire County Library, and the National Library of Wales at Aberystwyth.

Finally, as the late Alexander Cordell once said to me, 'No one person ever writes a book.' Over the years, how true I have proved that to be. And, in this case especially, as so often, it would certainly not have been possible without the patience, support, proof-reading, constructive criticism and understanding of a long-suffering wife.

Having said all of which, I would say a very sincere word of thanks for the wholehearted enthusiasm and encouragement right from the start of the publishers and, remembering that the man who never made a mistake never made anything, need only add that any mistakes will be all my own work.

Roscoe Howells

Picture Credits

P51 Bill Frost and his workmen:
courtesy Mrs Olive Frost

P54 All three pictures: Margaret Howells

Pp 56 & 57 All four pictures: Margaret Howells

P58 Griffithston Hill: Margaret Howells
Griffithston Lane: Alan Shepherd

P59 Storm damage in Tenby harbour:
courtesy Pembrokeshire Records Office

Pp 60 & 61 All five pictures: Mel Davies

P62 Mrs Ena Mortimer: Author

P.64 Long distance view with points identified:
Alan Shepherd

Foreword

For those of us born and brought up in Saundersfoot, it has been no more than an accepted fact of life that a man by the name of Bill Frost, a native of the village, built and flew an aeroplane before the end of the 19th century.

Inevitably there have been those who have known only part of the story, and many more from other places unable to believe any of it.

There are few still living who knew Bill Frost, and fewer still with the knowledge to tell his story and ensure that it would not be lost for all time.

Roscoe Howells, himself a true 'Sandersfooter', has more than close local and personal knowledge to justify his writing such a book as this. Not only has he known so many of those of whom he writes, including Bill Frost himself, quoting some of their stories, but as a reputed local historian has shown in his many books on Pembrokeshire that he has ever been thorough and diligent in his research. Written in the author's familiar and easy style, this book is no exception and is certain to give real pleasure to a host of fascinated readers.

Donald Johns
Chairman, Saundersfoot Historical Society.

Chapter 1

The First Flight

Late in the month of September, 1896, William Frost, more usually known at the time, and now increasingly to history, as Bill Frost, built his flying machine and flew it from Griffithston Hill overlooking what was then the small fishing and coal-exporting village of Saundersfoot in South Pembrokeshire in the far west of Wales.

That fact having been established will mean that the history books will have to be rewritten, but that is something which is always in danger of happening in any walk of life. Scientists and researchers are doing it all the time.

Watched by no more than a few of his family and a near neighbour or two, he took off from the field at Griffithston Hill and travelled a distance of certainly more than five hundred yards. For how many seconds he had been airborne it would be difficult to say, but it was for a distance of some hundreds of yards, before, in trying to clear the hedge, the undercarriage caught in a tree and the machine came down in the brambles. That night a storm was to destroy Bill Frost's dreams and his work of years. More than a century later the oak tree where he came to grief is still there.

For fifteen years he had been working on his plans and experiments, by which time he was forty-seven years of age, and had been a widower for the last seven of them.

The *Tenby and County News* of October 9th, 1895, carried a brief news item which said, 'Mr William Frost, Saundersfoot, has obtained provisional protection for a new flying machine, invented by him, and is supplying the designs necessary to secure a patent. Two motive powers are employed, gas and a horizontal fan. The inventor confidently predicts a speed of 100 miles per hour for the first start. He has been engaged on the machine over 15 years, and is satisfied that the difficulties of aerial navigation have been surmounted by him.'

Two days later, on Friday, October 11th, in its Saundersfoot column, the *Pembrokeshire Herald and General Advertiser* carried the same story, word for word.

Apart from those two newspaper entries, for more than three decades there would seem to have been little enough committed to paper concerning this event, but more recently other documents have come to light.

Bill Frost submitted his Provisional Specification of his Flying Machine on October 25th, 1894.

'William Frost Carpenter and Builder Saundersfoot Pembrokeshire do hereby declare the nature of this invention to be as follows:

The flying machine is propelled into the air by two reversible fans revolving horizontally. When sufficient height is gained, wings are spread and tilted by means of a lever, causing the machine to float onward and upward. When low enough the lever is reversed causing it to rise upward & onward. When required to stop it the wings are tilted so as to hold against the wind or air and lowered by the reversible fans. The steering is done by a

helm fitted to front of machine.
October 25th, 1894.   William Frost.'

The following year, 1895, on August 30th, Bill Frost submitted the final specification and drawings for his machine. The patent was registered in the December, under the reference number 20,431/94, and by the following September, 1896, Bill Frost was ready to fly.

Chapter 2

The Storm

At the sudden, and as it transpired, tragic end to that first brief flight, apart from the considerable discomfort of having come down in the brambles, Bill Frost was not unduly injured, nor did the machine sustain any irreparable damage.

Fate, however, was against him. That night, before he could set about retrieving the machine in order to repair such damage as it had sustained, and prepare for a further attempt, there came one of the typical equinoctial storms which were to hit Pembrokeshire during the autumn on several occasions in the 1890's.

In an epic of which so little has been recorded, it is here that we have to look for some confirmation of the date. There have been suggestions that it could have taken place in 1895, and the Complete Specification had indeed been finally accepted on October 19th of that year. We do, however, have Bill Frost's word that it happened in September, and it is permissible to ask whether he would have flown his machine before the October in anticipation of the patent being granted and finally approved, or whether he would have waited until he knew his design and plans had been protected.

Even the local newspapers of those days regarded it as part of their function to disseminate news from all over the world, so we can be sure that Bill Frost knew something of what others were trying to do. To him, simple village carpenter though he was, it would no doubt have occurred to him as being no more than ordinary common sense to ensure, first of all, that his patent had been protected. Then, when at last it had received the Royal Seal, he could have felt it was safe to press on with his venture and be ready for the first flight in the autumn of 1896, and this is most certainly what he did.

There were some fierce storms in the autumn of 1895, with reports of shipwrecks and damage to property all round the Pembrokeshire coast. There are many revealing pictures to act as a permanent reminder of the ferocity of the gales and the extent of the damage, which are far more telling than any mere words could ever be.

When we read of the shipwrecks round the Pembrokeshire coast in the autumn of 1895, we can think of how the great wooden ships in days of sail were driven before the storms on the surface of the water, and then appreciate that Bill Frost's flimsy machine, with any sort of wind behind it, would have been no more than so much chaff.

Writing of Bill Frost, in a well-researched, but necessarily brief article, in the 1985 September/October issue of *Air-Britain Digest*, Paul Williams expressed the opinion that the likely year was 1896, and he was unquestionably correct in his assumption. He referred to a newspaper article of 1932 when Frost, then eighty-four years of age, who had unfortunately not given the year, was quoted as having said that it was in September, and we know that as early as September in the year 1896 there was a great storm.

The *Tenby and County News* gave a full report on it in its

edition of Wednesday, September 30th, under the heading:

'Great Storm:
A tremendous storm swept over South Wales on Friday, doing much damage to property, and playing havoc in a number of other directions.'

A fortnight later, the same paper carried the headlines,

'Great Gale at Tenby
A Breach in Tenby Pier
Great Destruction Of Property
The Lifeboat Out Nearly All Day
The Rocket To The Rescue
£1,500 Damage To Tenby Pier
Rescue Of Twenty-One Lives'

Similar damage was reported at Saundersfoot, and there are pictures to show what happened at Tenby harbour.

To this extent we are fortunate that, although photography was in its infancy, there were Tenby pioneers in that field in the persons of Charles Smith Allen, and his two sons, H. Mortimer Allen and Samuel J. Allen. They left a precious legacy for those interested in the history of the area, and many of their pictures have been, and are still being, reproduced in book form from time to time by those who publish books on Pembrokeshire.

Why is it, then, it is reasonable to ask, that the pioneering Allens failed to record such an historic event as Bill Frost's crashed 'plane? That is the first question the sceptics ask, and a very reasonable question it is indeed a century later, especially in an age when we hear of the gentlemen of the paparazzi having been on the scene of many a news headline story almost before it has happened.

It is difficult to think of a suitable analogy to place the question in perspective in the context of anything which might happen today. All sorts of cranks have forever been, and still are, doing all sorts of daft and crazy things all over the world. Unless there has been some astute or high-powered advance publicity, the antics of such cranks do not usually make news until after they have happened. In today's parlance, Bill Frost's flight was strictly a non-event. Had he cleared the tree it would have been an entirely different matter.

It was enough for the pioneering photographers of the day, with their great tripods and glass plates, to be taking pictures of buildings, which had only ever until that time been seen in paintings or sketches, and to be lining up people for group pictures, with instructions to stand perfectly still and to 'watch the dicky-bird'. With memorable pictures of broken ships to be taken where they had been hurled up onto the battered walls of Tenby harbour, there would never have been any question of travelling three miles by pony-and-trap to Saundersfoot, carrying cumbersome photographic equipment, to take pictures of the wreck of some crazy person's creation, apart from the fact that, for all practical purposes, by the time the news reached Tenby the flying machine would have been no more.

Nor, in the face of the general overall havoc wrought by the storm, would a virtually unknown Bill Frost's personal tragedy have been of any consequence or news value whatsoever. As far as many local people were concerned, the poor chap had gone off his head anyway, and to their way of thinking they had good grounds for saying so. In all conscience, he had experienced more than enough trouble for people to have been at least partially justified in thinking it.

It had to be left to those who really knew about his efforts at the time to pass the word down to succeeding generations.

The story has been told throughout the years in the Saundersfoot area, and it is well-known what happened as a result of the fearful storm, which blew up on the night of Bill Frost's flight, after his machine had landed in the brambles. Whilst any sort of strong wind would no doubt have been enough to lift the flimsy machine, that night the south-westerly gale hurled at least part of the machine far down to a field by the name of Steart in the valley below. What the name means, or whether it is even the correct spelling, it would be difficult to say. It would appear to be a corruption of the name Sload, under which it was entered on a map of 1839, the meaning of which is also obscure. There could have been no question of trying to salvage the scattered wreckage, and certainly not of trying to reassemble it.

The machine had come down in the Well Field, known by that name because there was, and possibly still is, a well of lovely water there. The whole approach to the place has long since been overgrown and become almost impenetrable. Part of the wreckage was to remain there for years and, for all we know, could still be there.

Chapter 3

The Quest Of Icarus

How much Bill Frost is likely to have read of those who had made attempts before ever he tried to take to the air by powered flight we do not know, but certainly man's ambition had been there for a long time.

Conquest of the air had been a long-cherished dream, and many a schoolboy, in the days when children were educated, could no doubt have quoted his mythology if asked who had been the first man to fly. A great story it was about Daedalus, the legendary constructor of the Labyrinth of Crete, and his son, Icarus, who were imprisoned by Minos, the king.

Whilst the thought of living on an island appeals to many, surfeiting, the appetite may sicken, as Shakespeare had it to be about music, and after a while Daedalus planned their escape. A great idea it was to be sure, with wings made of feathers and stuck together by wax, but Daedalus warned his son not to fly too high lest the wax should be in danger of melting in the heat of the sun. Ever since time began, however, sons have had a habit of heeding not their father's advice, and the youthful Icarus was no exception. Rejoicing in his new-found freedom he soared high, high aloft like the voice of Nedda, the soprano in Leoncavallo's *Pagliacci*, as she vied with the birds high, high aloft in their beautiful singing, and the poor father's worst fears were realised. The wax melted, his wayward son plunged into the sea and was drowned.

How much of the story is pure legend, and how much could have been founded on fact, we are never likely to know, but it is nice to think, especially with such a sad end to the tale, that Daedalus and Icarus might have been the first men on record to use gliders. If they were, then it is fairly certain that it would have been as the result of a careful study of air currents and the possibility of riding them on wings in the same way as the birds.

Nor do we need to go as far as Crete in search of legend. There was the story of Bladud, the king, who founded the city of Bath something like three thousand years ago, long before the Romans came. According to Geoffrey of Monmouth he was killed when making an experiment in flying in 852 BC. He was said to have fallen upon the temple of his god, Apolyn in the city of Trinovantum, which is to say London, and, hardly surprisingly at that time, Bladud's aspirations to 'flie into y ayer' were attributed to necromancy and a false 'pryde and presumpcion'.

According to Milton, two thousand years later, there was a character by the name of Oliver of Malemsbury who, 'in his youth strangely aspiring, had made and fitted Wings to his Hands and Feet; with these on the top of a Tower, spread out to gather air, he flew more than a furlong; but the wind being too high, came fluttering down to the maiming of his limbs; yet so conceited of his Art, that he attributed the cause of his fall to the want of a Tail, as Birds have, which he forgot to make to his hinder parts.'

There were many other references long ago to the possibility of flight by men, who seem to have lacked nothing by way of ideas, but, like Bill Frost of a later generation, only the means, and no doubt the encouragement, to develop them. 17th Century literature is full of fanciful references to the possibility of flight, both by balloon as well as by 'wing'. A certain Bishop Wilkins thought that the three main objections to the possibility of man ever flying were the natural heaviness of a man's body, the extreme coldness of the air at the higher altitudes, and the thinness of the upper air, but he believed that if men could ever fly upwards for twenty miles, then the force of gravity would be overcome, and man might stand as firmly in the open air as upon the ground.

Moving from the world of legend to that of reality we find as long ago as 1742 a flying experiment conducted by the Marquis of Bacqueville in Paris in sight of a great crowd. He used what was known as Besnier's flying apparatus, which was an apparatus used for gliding, named after Besnier, a locksmith who had invented it in 1676.

Consisting of two rods, each with a hinged plane at either end, the apparatus was carried on the shoulders. The supporting surfaces could be made to open and shut like a book, with the feet being attached to the back planes in order to make them open and shut as required.

The Marquis was one of many who tried to improve on the idea, and eventually he launched himself from the roof of his riverside mansion to glide across the Seine towards the Tuileries, where he hoped to land in the gardens. He failed to reach that far and fell on to the barges used by the laundresses at the Pont Royal and injured himself badly.

Amusing as such efforts may be to those who look back from the achievements of this supersonic age, at least their efforts showed the way to those who were to follow them. It is believed by many that the remarkable Italian genius, Leonardo da Vinci, was the true discoverer of the principles and practice of flight at the beginning of the 16th Century.

Another Italian, by the name of Borelli, who lived some hundreds of years ago, also demonstrated the possibilities of artificial wings or planes.

Whilst the Frenchman, Paucton, in the 18th Century, was describing a machine with two propellers, Sir George Cayley, in the summer of 1853, was giving a practical demonstration at Brompton-by-Sawdon, in Yorkshire, of some of his theories which at least showed that he had a clear understanding of the principles of flight by aeroplane. His glider was reproduced and placed on display at the Science Museum in South Kensington.

In 1843, five years before the birth of Bill Frost, a group of industrial pioneers believed that the prospects looked so good that they felt justified in seeking Parliamentary powers for the Aerial Steam Transit Company. Although the Bill survived its first reading, the public were unenthusiastic and no significant amount of capital was raised.

Henson, one of the group, had an aerostat which was considered to represent a serious attempt at aviation on a significant scale. Two of the group, Stringfellow and Wenham, with less elaborate ideas, carried the concept of flight a stage further, and Wenham designed a simple model, fitted with an engine, for which he was awarded a prize of £100 at the Exhibition of the Aeronautical Society of Great Britain at the Crystal Palace in 1868.

Another who had to work with steam for his motive power, before the coming of the internal combustion engine, was an Englishman, Thomas Moy. Whatever the steam engine offered by way of driving power, however, it sacrificed in weight and clumsiness of design. Moy recognised this and, in designing his so-called aerial steamer, did away with the idea of a boiler, proposing to use a new and fairly light engine to achieve the necessary velocity for the initial run over the ground. He believed that the weight of the engine would gradually be thrown upon the 'plane in the same way that the weight of larger birds, such as eagles, was thrown upon their wings after a few preliminary hops. This effort, too, resulted in failure.

At the same time, in the 1890's, a leading inventor in America, who was eventually to become famous in Britain as Sir Hiras Maxim, along with a fellow American, Professor Langley, experimented with large and small steam-driven models. Yet, although they had the support of a large staff of skilled workmen, they failed in the end, although Maxim went near to a limited success in England.

The race to be first in the air continued, and the honour went officially to the Americans, Wilbur and Orville Wright, for their historic flight at Kitty Hawk in December, 1903. The Wright brothers, too, had met with the usual scepticism, and experienced much frustration, but at least they found adequate financial support eventually and, profiting from the mistakes and experience of other pioneers in the same field, went on to greater success and honour following their initial breakthrough.

Bill Frost, the humble carpenter, working on his own in a remote corner in the south of Pembrokeshire, far, far away in West Wales, had no such support, financial or technical, or anyone to whom he could turn for advice. Unhonoured and unsung, at the time when the outside world knew nothing of him or his efforts, he had beaten the Wright brothers to it by seven years and three months.

Chapter 4

Who Was Bill Frost?

William Frost was born in Saundersfoot on May 28th, 1848, the son of John Frost and his wife, Rebecca.

These days such an event, together with details of the family background, would perhaps rate more than a line or two, plus the obligatory picture, in the tabloids. But the tabloids were not with us at that time, nor even the pioneering Allen photographer family.

It has long been understood amongst the Frost family that John Frost was related to John Frost, the celebrated Chartist leader of Newport, who died in 1877, and was buried at St Edmund's Church, Harfield, Bristol. The exact relationship has not yet been established and, whilst of passing interest, is by no means essential to the telling of Bill Frost's story.

All that is known of the John Frost who eventually came to Saundersfoot is that he was born c.1771 in the Aberystwyth area, and that his father, William, had been a miner. It would be well within the bounds of possibility that he could have moved there to work in one of the lead, silver or gold mines operating in that area at the time. That would not have been surprising if, like his Chartist relation, he had come from the strong mining area of Monmouthshire.

Although there is no authenticated reference, it has been said in the family that John, as a young man, was referred to as a guardsman in the militia, as a result of which his service brought him in the year 1797 to Fishguard, in the north of Pembrokeshire, where he was involved in the defence of the realm on the occasion of the historic last invasion of Britain by the French, which momentous episode in the annals of the Premier County has been fully chronicled over the years.

The family having apparently moved west from Monmouthshire to Aberystwyth, and John having moved south to Fishguard, his next move would seem to have been southwards again, because when he married Rebecca, the daughter of Lewis and Mary Nash, on August 25th, 1844, he was a widower and given as a confectioner in the town of Tenby, whilst Rebecca was a spinster, and there is nothing unusual in that, either then or now, which is to say when folk bother to get married at all. The Nashes were an old Saundersfoot family, and Rebecca's father was also a miner. Although the older type of pit had been in operation in the area for many years, Lewis Nash would probably have been working in the nearby Bonville's Court pit, which had been sunk two years earlier, in 1842. The Nash family were living then at Griffithston, the area on the other side of the valley from Bonville's Court, and which was the area where Bill Frost would later live for a time, and from which he would eventually fly his machine.

The 1841 Census gives John Frost as a pastry cook, living with his wife, Mary, at St Julian Street, Tenby. Both of them were given as seventy years of age but, for the purposes of that Census, ages were rounded up or down to the nearest five years. When Mary died in January, 1844, at Bridge Street, she was seventy-six, and it was in the August of that year John Frost married Rebecca.

There would have been nothing about any of this to whet the appetite of the devotees of the tabloids, however, until we come to notice that John was seventy-three when he married Rebecca, whilst she was a mere twenty-one, which is where the story might just raise the eyebrows a little.

Contrary to whatever might have been anticipated, John and Rebecca had six children, and John lived on until he died at the age of eighty-nine in 1861. Of the six children, the only two with whom we are concerned are William, born in 1848, and his sister, Sarah, born thirteen years later, in the year their father died in his ninetieth year.

In the early years of their marriage John and Rebecca were shown in the Census Returns as living at Clift Cottage, which was in the village in Wogan Street, Clift being the Pembrokeshire word for Cliff. John was still working at his trade as a baker. By the time he died, in 1861, the family had moved to a cottage at Hopshill, which was near to Griffithston. He would seem to have held some land there, because when, in 1899, Bill Frost married for the second time, his father was given as having been a farmer. There would have been nothing unusual about that. The Census Returns for that age show an abundance of such entries for smallholders who worked at all sorts of rural occupations, particularly miners or colliers in that area, as well as shoemakers, tailors, roadmen, blacksmiths, builders or, in the case of the Frost family, carpenters or even pastry cook or baker. With a small acreage, a few cows and young stock, as well as sometimes a horse, a man would as often as not be entered as a farmer no matter what his other, and perhaps main, occupation might be.

For whatever reason, at the time of Bill Frost's first marriage, John was given as having been a collier. Whatever the reason for the discrepancies, however, it was as a pastry cook or confectioner he had been shown on the various Census Returns, as well as on the occasion of his marriage to Rebecca.

Sometime during the ensuing decade, following John's death, Rebecca married a widower, Jeremiah Davies, and in 1871 they were living at Griffithston Hill, together with the children of both marriages, including William, who was shown as a carpenter, and Sarah. When Rebecca died, in 1902, she was buried at Bethesda in the same grave as Jeremiah, who had died in 1875. The stone also commemorated her first husband, John Frost, who had been buried at St Issell's churchyard. His age on the stone is given, for some reason or other, as having been seventy-eight, but the burial register of St Issell's quite clearly gives him as having been eighty-nine at the time of his death, and the 1851 Census, taken ten years earlier, had given him as being eighty.

The Census of 1871 would also have been taken about April and, on July 15th that year, at the Calvinistic Methodist Chapel, otherwise known as the Presbyterian, at Bethesda, shortly after he had been shown as a single man living with his mother, Bill Frost, at the age of twenty-three, married twenty-one years old Margaretta Thomas of nearby Bonville's Court, whose father, James, was also given as a carpenter. It is not known where Bill Frost had learned his trade but, although that can only be a matter for conjecture, it is perhaps permissible to wonder whether it could have been with his future father-in-law.

Bill Frost and Margaretta would seem to have made their first home in the village itself, for the 1881 Census gives them as living at Railway Street, euphemistically referred to these days as The Strand, because there has been a remarkable propensity for people over the years to change the names of roads, and especially houses, and the fashion persists to this day. But Railway Street it will always be to those of an older generation. It was there that the railway, with its horse-drawn drams, had run from the 1840's, bringing coal from the pits at Stepaside to the recently built Saundersfoot harbour. In the 1870's a new line was laid and the horses were replaced by the *Rosalind*, the little engine, which ran until the 1930's, and which will ever be affectionately remembered by those who were fascinated by her in their childhood.

Of no relevance to the epic of Bill Frost and his flying machine, but of perhaps more than passing interest to those with an interest in local history, would be the fact that one of the Frosts' near neighbours, at 18 Railway Street, in the 1880's would have been the former Mary Prout, who had been imprisoned for having thrown her baby down a pit in Amroth parish, and whose story was told in full in the book *From Amroth to Utah*, (Gomer 2001).

Bill and Margaretta Frost were shown in the 1881 Census as living at 8-9 Railway Street, which in itself does not tell us very much. When we come to the 1891 Census Returns we are confronted by a salutary reminder of what life really must have been like for the poorer working people in those days, because, for the first time, the Census gives the number of rooms where there had been fewer than five rooms in a house. Then we realise that, in the Census figures for earlier years, families of twelve or more would have been living, not, as might have been thought, in separate cottages all bearing the same name, but in two-roomed squalor and all sleeping in the one room.

The Frost's first child, Edith, was born in 1872. The following year another daughter, Ethel, was born and died at the age of one month. After that came a boy, Wilfred, and then came another daughter, and she, too, was named Ethel after the little one who had died so young. It was a common

28

practice in those days of high mortality among children to name a child after one who had died, and the registers are full of such examples. There was a firm commitment to the philosophy of Job, 'The Lord gave and the Lord hath taken back, blessed be the name of the Lord. If we take happiness from the hand of the Lord, should we not take sorrow, too?' After Ethel came another boy, Lawson.

In 1887, the first-born child, Edith, died at the age of fifteen, and then, three months later, Margaretta died at the age of thirty-seven. By this time Bill Frost's mother, now Rebecca Davies, was once again a widow, holding enough land, eighteen acres in fact, to be entered in the 1891 Census as a small farmer, and her bereaved son had moved back with his young family of three children to live with her and the rest of the family at Griffithston Hill. Small wonder that in the light of his experiments in the ensuing years there were those who thought that the poor man had gone off his head.

Wilfred, the older of the two boys, was already working alongside his father, learning his trade as a carpenter. Meanwhile, Bill Frost's younger sister, Sarah, had married a man by the name of William Watkins, and in due course they, too, would eventually live at Griffithston Hill.

Some years after this, in 1899, Bill Frost married a single woman by the name of Annie Griffiths and moved into her home in St Bride's Lane, at which point it is necessary to digress slightly to learn something of the Griffiths family if the background to the story of Bill Frost, as here being told, is to be fully appreciated. It was where she had been born, and it had been the family home for generations. She had three older brothers, Isaac being the eldest, then Jim, and John, who was the youngest. All three were carpenters. John's son, another John, known as Jack Griffiths, had been a young boy when Bill Frost flew his plane. Jack Griffiths, too, was a carpenter, whose work was beyond compare, and who became a legend in his own lifetime. Nobody with any sense would do more than look at his cherished tools, let alone touch them or ask to borrow them. He and his son, Mark, who had learned his trade alongside his father, worked with my father for years. At one time the carpenter's shop was a lean-to in our garden at the pine-end at the back of the Bethany Chapel.

As a small boy, I spent hours with Mr Griffiths, and when one of our hens, named Maimi, died, there had to be a proper committal at the bottom of the garden with a wooden cross to mark the sacred place. Maybe the wooden cross was only made of lath, but that was no reason for it not to be properly bevelled and jointed and planed. Then he took his carpenter's pencil from behind his ear and we discussed the epitaph. To my small boy's mind it was the poetry of a genius when he wrote on it that the cause of death was 'Stoppage of the heart'.

Occasionally I would go up to their house for tea, and what a treat that was when Mrs Griffiths would give me bread and butter with sugar on it. To her, a child of the 'Hungry Nineties', reared as one of seven children in a three-roomed cottage and out in service by the time she was twelve, that would have been luxury indeed. Jam, if they ever had it in her childhood, would have been from fruit in season, and not something bought from a shop.

Sometimes to walk up to the Griffiths' home at Plantation Cottages I would go up St Bride's Lane past the Frosts' home, where Bill Frost's workshop was just off the road. An old converted 'clom' cottage it was, with the wall having been opened up to make one big room of it. Heedful of the changing of names over the years, it should be said that at that time their home was known as Stammers Cottage, and it was there that I perhaps remember Bill Frost best of all, because from 1929 onwards, until his death in 1935, that was where he was when we lived next-door to him, and I spent many of my boyhood hours with him and his wife.

Before that, however, he had been the Sunday School Superintendent at the Bethany Chapel where, in her earlier days, my mother had been a Sunday School teacher. It was because of this that my parents had the tenancy of the Bethany Manse, now the Jalna Hotel, next-door to the chapel, and it was there that my mother died in childbirth when I was born in 1919.

Ten years later my father built a house, Merlewood, at the top of St Bride's Hill. Like the Bethany Manse, that, too, has now been extended to become a hotel. Bill Frost's orchard and cottage were the other side of the hedge. The cottage has long since been demolished and the orchard built on.

In spite of the bitter disappointment which was to be his unfortunate lot, in later years, when he was to become blind and die a virtual pauper, his spirit was to remain undimmed.

Apart from any of his inventive skills and ability at his trade, he was also a fine musician, who even played an old-fashioned type of banjolele. Whilst the invention of his flying machine remained a secret from the wider world for so long, a possibly bigger secret, albeit of considerably less importance, was the fact that his banjolele was my introduction to a musical instrument so popular at the time. Whilst I would not claim that the dear old gentleman taught me to play it, he at least viewed with amusement my first fumbling attempts at fingering. It was later that I acquired the real interest and some reasonable proficiency on the instrument. Sufficient at any rate to have appeared in cabaret at the London Lyceum. And if the people who

31

would question whether Bill Frost really did fly, would wish to question that as well, I can give them the date. It was in a special charity show for the Metropolitan Police London Welsh Society on September 26th, 1969.

From time to time there would be a reference in the local papers to Bill Frost and his musical doings. In the *Narberth Weekly News* of June 3rd, 1926, for example, we read that James Thomas, the famous Welsh Bard known as 'Iago', was visiting the village. Then, on July 8th, the same newspaper carried a brief item which said, 'Boatmen casting one morning last week were attracted by singing, and on investigation, found two old veterans tuning up in the brilliant sunshine. The two songsters turned out to be Mr James Thomas ('Iago') and Mr Wm Frost, and in the words of the boatmen, 'It sounded fine. Mr & Mrs Thomas left for their home at Treherbert on Tuesday last.'

Two years later, the *Tenby Observer*, sister paper to the *Narberth Weekly News*, in its issue of May 31st, 1928, carried a short report in its Saundersfoot column:

'Congratulations! – Heartiest congratulations to Mr William Frost, who on Sunday last attained his 80th birthday. A founder and conductor of Saundersfoot Male Voice Choir, Mr Frost last Sunday sat in the 'Sêt Fawr' of Bethany Presbyterian Church, and at the evening service was accompanied by 'Iago Blaen Rhondda', the famous Welsh bard. In a striking tribute to his great friend, Iago remarked that the singing of Mr Frost that day was to him an inspiration, and immediately he ventured into the realms of verse giving proof of same. For over sixty years Mr Frost has evinced a deep interest in the welfare of Bethany, and his contribution to the musical realms has always been keenly appreciated.'

He had also sung and recited at the anniversary service in the afternoon.

Whilst the more discerning reader will readily have understood that the great Iago was not Longfellow's character, he the greatest of all story-tellers, what could perhaps be of more interest is the use of the Welsh term 'Sêt Fawr' in this essentially English-speaking area in the heart of Little England Beyond Wales. Not that we are anything but Welsh to the core, other than in language, with a dialect of our own, even though it has all but died out. By tradition and culture we are the same, and shout as fervently as anybody when Wales take the field against England in a rugby international. Indeed, so truly Celtic are we, that we also shout for Scotland or Ireland, and especially Ireland, when the opposition is English. The 'Sêt Fawr' was the Big Seat, where the highly exalted characters in the persons of the deacons or elders themselves were privileged to sit.

Seven years later, when Bill Frost died a couple of months short of his eighty-seventh birthday, the same newspaper, in a report of his death, said, 'In his early days he was a vocalist and musician of considerable ability. Under his leadership the Saundersfoot Male Voice Party captured many notable choral victories on the eisteddfod platform in Pembrokeshire and Carmarthenshire, Mr Frost's favourite test piece being 'The Psalm of Life.'

Chapter 5

How It Began

However much or little Bill Frost might have heard of other people's efforts, he is quoted as having said that the conviction that man really would eventually be able to fly came to him when he was carrying a piece of timber in a strong wind and suddenly found himself airborne for a few seconds.

Here again, there could be some confusion about dates and ages, because an old newspaper report, to which reference can be made later, said that Bill Frost was still in his 'teens' when it happened, which would have been in the 1860's. Well, he was not. He was a young married man of twenty-eight when it happened in 1876.

As we grow older we become ever more and more aware that memory can play funny tricks. Bill Frost had made that statement himself, about being in his teens, to a newspaper reporter in 1932. But at that time he was eighty-four years of age and, after all the disappointments, and all the thought and work and money and time he had put into what should perhaps have been a world-famous venture, he could be forgiven for having been just a shade wide of the mark.

As we have seen, by 1876 he was married to Margaretta,

and they were living with their young family in Railway Street. We know it was 1876 because, when the wind had presumably struck the piece of timber at a certain angle, and the idea of man eventually being able to fly had come to him, he was working at Hean Castle, and here again a certain digression might be justified, especially when it is asked how Bill Frost could have had access to such materials as he would have required in such a remote and rural corner of the world.

In that year he was working as a carpenter on the rebuilding of Hean Castle, in an exposed situation overlooking the lovely Carmarthen Bay and Saundersfoot harbour, for the industrialist, Charles Ranken Vickerman, who was the leading light and the great driving force in the industrial development of the area.

People who come to the area these days find it difficult to envisage the industrial nature of Saundersfoot in bygone days, and how the harbour, built between 1829 and 1833, now packed with pleasure craft, could have been the scene of bustling activity as the sailing ships, and eventually the small steam ships, came in to load the world famous coal from Bonville's Court colliery, and from the Grove pit and the Lower Level pit at Stepaside. Nor is the term 'world famous' used lightly. It was a cause for great pride locally when Saundersfoot anthracite was used on the Royal Yacht. Subsequently, so impressed was Queen Victoria with its smoke-free qualities, that she decreed that no other coal should be used when she was on board.

The ambitious development of the harbour and in the coal industry, which included the pit at Bonville's Court, had been carried out by the Philipps family of the great Picton Castle Estate, and 'great' was the name for it in those days. As the late Francis Jones, Wales Herald Extraordinary, said in *Treasury Of Historic Pembrokeshire* (Brawdy Books,

1998), when referring to the Philippses of Picton, 'At one time the family owned nearly a third of the county of Pembroke, besides land in Cardiganshire and Carmarthenshire. In the last century they owned over twenty-two parishes.'

John Vickerman, a wealthy London solicitor, with an estate in Essex, was the solicitor to Lord Milford, one of the Philipps family, and it was through this connection that John's son, Charles Ranken Vickerman, became involved.

Nor was it only the coal which interested him. For many years prior to the early 19th Century iron ore had been extracted from the cliffs all the way along the coast from Saundersfoot to Amroth and exported by open boat from the beaches. In the early 1840's, at the same time as the sinking of the pit at Bonville's Court, Vickerman conceived the idea of further exploiting this mineral source, and built the ironworks adjoining the Grove pit at Stepaside. The venture was to prove a complete financial disaster, the 'white elephant' of the ironworks being in production for no more than twelve years between its opening in the 1840's and its eventual closure in the late 1870's. The iron ore, or 'mine' as it was called, was dug from the cliffs between Amroth and Wisemansbridge, known as Crickdam, where the remains of a cottage and a blacksmith's shop can still be seen.

At Woodside, near Wisemansbridge, there was an iron foundry and a brickworks. The railway line which ran along the foot of the cliffs, and passed through three tunnels, from Saundersfoot to Stepaside had already come into being, and Saundersfoot harbour was due to become a busy little port indeed in those brave days of sail.

The full history of these various developments has been told in M.R.C. Price's splendid book, *Industrial Saundersfoot* (Gomer 1982), and in my own book, *Old Saundersfoot*

(Gomer 1977). The story in my novel, *Crickdam* (Gomer 1990), is also set against the factual historical background of that time.

As the various enterprises failed, the industrial era finally came to an end with the closing of Bonville's Court colliery, with its notoriously faulty coal seams, in 1932. For all that he had been due to lose a fortune in these ventures, Vickerman was originally a wealthy power in the land, and in 1869 he bought Hean Castle, which had been the home of Thomas Stokes, a former industrialist on a smaller scale.

In 1876, bringing in red sandstone from Cheshire as ballast for the sailing ships coming in to Saundersfoot harbour, Vickerman set about the rebuilding of the ancient house known as Hean Castle, and Bill Frost worked there as a carpenter. The rest is history.

How long it took him to work out his plans, or what ideas passed through his fertile mind following that day when he had become airborne, we shall probably never know, but we have seen that he was close enough to all the industrial activity taking place throughout the area for us to realise that the canvas used in the sailing ships would have been readily available and suitable in some form or other for covering material for the wings of his machine. The pits and ironworks, too, would no doubt have given him his ideas for the use and availability of the sheet metal for the fans.

Whilst, as far as possible, we have to stick to such facts as we have and to what has been handed down to us verbally, where it is necessary to conjecture at all, it is permissible to speculate on this technical point. Whatever the manufactured materials he eventually decided to use, they would have been readily obtainable in the area at that time.

No doubt there would also have been the vitally

important question of the right sort of timber for the framework. All we know is that Bill Frost said he had been carrying a piece of light timber on his shoulder when he became airborne and the idea had come to him, so quite possibly it could have been alder, or maybe a piece of flooring-board. Whatever it was, he would have had plenty of scope to seek it out in the wooded valley near which he lived.

As we have seen, at that time he was living in Railway Street. He could possibly have begun thinking about his plans soon afterwards, but it is doubtful whether he would have started on his practical experiments immediately. Not only was he a young married man with a wife and small family to support, but neither was it an age when the working class had a great deal of spare time on their hands for indulging themselves in such fond and foolish notions as going where no man had gone before. Understandably, with financial support from none, it must have taken him many long hours, and patient and weary days and years, before he could possibly have been ready to put his final ideas and creation to the ultimate test.

We know that on the death of Margaretta in 1888 he moved back to his mother's home at Griffithston Hill. There are various entries in the Census Returns and other records, but there is not always uniformity over the names of the various dwellings. We find Griffithston Hill, sometimes plain Griffithston, and there was also Griffithston Cottage. Somewhere about this time, Bill Frost's sister, Sarah, thirteen years younger than he was, had married a man by the name of William Watkins and, in 1891, was living at Broadfield Cottage, when William was employed as a gardener. Probably on the death of her mother, Rebecca, in 1902, or shortly afterwards, Sarah would have moved back to Griffithston Hill with her own family. Sarah's grand-daughter, Josie Watkins, still lives there.

The two cottages, known as Griffithston Cottages, were down the field below Griffithston Hill in what was known as Griffithston Lane, so perhaps a word of caution could be of help to those who think they know the area when they try to puzzle out the exact location of Bill Frost's activities. Today there is a sign at this part of suburbia which says that it is Ragged Staff. It never was, so cannot be so now. It was, and therefore is, Griffithston Lane.

Ragged Staff, which now has a name-plate to proclaim that it is Stammers Road, started near the bottom of St Bride's Hill, and ran up to what was referred to as the crossroads, but which is really a junction with the road running up from Rhodewood to Sandy Hill. The Bethany Manse was a hundred yards or so from the junction with St Bride's Hill, and our address was Bethany Manse, Ragged Staff, Saundersfoot. We did not run to a postcode at that time, but any letters found us, and with a good deal earlier delivery than we have today. The area known as Stammers Mountain, as clearly defined on the map of 1839, was to the left of anyone going up Ragged Staff. Griffithston Hill was the area below that and where Ragged Staff ran. It was one good reason why the cottage up St Bride's Lane, where Bill Frost lived with his second wife and spent his last years, was known as Stammers Cottage.

I said earlier that it was understandable that people might have considered that Bill Frost was going off his head and attributed it to the personal tragedies he had known. My cousin, Ivor Howell, who was eight years older than I was, remembered well an occasion when the subject of Bill Frost's flying machine was being talked about, and his mother recounted an incident in her own youth, but we cannot put an exact date to it.

Born in 1874, she went into service at the age of twelve,

which was about par for the course, as the saying is, for those days. When she was fourteen, which was the time when Bill Frost's wife died, she went to work at St Andrew's, a private school in Tenby, and worked there until she married. So the incident to which she referred would have been after 1888, and probably when she was a young woman in the early 1890's. She and another girl were walking home to Wisemansbridge on their day off. Their road would normally have taken them via Twycross and Saundersfoot village by way of the tramroad through the tunnels. There had been talk in the area, however, of Bill Frost running round the field at Griffithston Hill holding a sheet of zinc, or some light metal or other, above his head and, when they reached Twycross, the girl with Ivor's mother said, 'Isn't it a pity about that poor man Frost gwain off his head. Let's go round Stammers and see what a's tryin' to do.' Which is one more good reason for having tried to spell out where places of the various names were in the days of which we are talking, and when we shall be considering the significance of what different people are quoted as having said.

The story, too, has often been told that Bill Frost had spent time studying birds in their flight at different times according to the strength of the wind, the direction in which it was blowing at different times, and any effect it would have on the birds in their flight. He would have been in an ideal position to do this on the hill top at Griffithston running about with his sheet of light metal, and with the gulls gliding overhead.

By the time Bill Frost came to make his attempted flight into the unknown, his fifteen-year-old son, Wilfred, as we have already seen, was working alongside him. To what extent he would have been involved in his father's work on the flying machine is not known, but it is reasonable to suppose that he would have passed on some word of it to his children.

Chapter 6

Our Fathers Have Told Us

'Remember the days of old, consider the years of many generations: ask thy father, and he will shew thee; thy elders and they will tell thee.' (Deuteronomy Ch.32, V.7)

In any account of what happened more than a hundred years ago, and where there is such a paucity of the written and recorded word, we have to rely heavily on the stories which have been passed down to us. Let us not forget that much of what is recorded in the Bible of the great events of the day was written down many, many years after it had been handed down by word of mouth from one generation to another.

This may seem strange to those of today's generation whose minds have to absorb so much of the pernicious garbage being spewed out day after day, and night after night, on the idiot's lantern. Time was when we would sit round the fire, by the light of the candle or a paraffin lamp, and listen again and again to the stories being told and passed on by those who had lived their lives before us. Electricity came to Saundersfoot in 1925 and, by the following autumn, the *Narberth Weekly News* was able to report that more than a hundred houses had been connected, but, after all life's vicissitudes and the hand which fate had dealt him, Bill Frost by that time was not amongst the elite of those who could afford it.

When stories are told and retold there is inevitably a slight variation or difference on points of fact, over who said what, or where and when they said it. It is generally accepted that when there are ten witnesses to an accident there are likely to be ten slightly different versions as to exactly what happened, but it does not alter the fact that there was an accident.

Or again, we can turn to the Bible to make the point. Passed on as they were by word of mouth for so many years before they were eventually written down, we find discrepancies even amongst the Gospels on points of detail, but never on points of fact.

As somebody or other once wrote, the only possible evidence for any historical fact after so many years is that the men of that day, who would have been the only ones in a position to judge the evidence, believed it and put it forth as an authoritative statement.

Not only did I know Bill Frost and hear him tell something of his own story but, ever since childhood, I have mixed with others who knew him, and have heard the subject of his flight referred to from time to time, as different people repeated slightly different versions of the same story, or expressed different opinions on what happened. Indeed, I have to admit that, although as a boy I heard the story from his own lips as he talked to my father, I had the vague idea from my own knowledge of the area that the route of his flight would have taken him out more over the valley than in the direction which he did in fact take, which was westwards towards Bethesda. But, whatever variations there may have been in the same story, never, never ever, have I heard of those who lived at the time and knew, being quoted as having said it was all a heap of nonsense and that

Bill Frost never flew.

True, there are plenty of people today, and very clever and well qualified people at that, who are prepared to say it could not have happened and that they cannot believe it, but they cannot quote any source as ever having said that it did not happen.

Come to think of it, I remember reading some years ago that highly qualified aeronautical engineers have proved conclusively that a bumble bee, with its inadequate wings in relation to the size and weight of its body, could not possibly fly. The bumble bee, knowing nothing of this conclusive proof, just flies away and manages to collect a fair bit of honey to add to the weight whilst doing it. I know I wrote a little piece about it somewhere at the time, but I cannot now remember where, and I don't suppose it really matters.

Discussion of the technical details of the machine, and the possibility of its having flown, however, have to be left to those who are qualified to deal with such a subject. For my own part, if pressed, I would have to admit that I could not tell the difference between a two-thread lug and a slot-side cam brace. I know only what I know. Speaking from my own knowledge and personal experience, I can only say that never from as far back as I can remember have I ever had cause to entertain the smallest shadow of a doubt as to whether or not Bill Frost flew.

Jack Griffiths, with whom I spent so much time in his carpenter's shop when I was a small boy, and who was the nephew of Mrs Annie Frost, was born in 1886, two years before the death of Bill Frost's first wife, Margaretta, so he would have been about ten years old when Bill Frost took to the air. Be sure that such an event would have made a huge, never-to-be-forgotten, impression on a boy of that age, especially one born and brought up as he had been at

Stammers Cottage, just a few hundred yards down the road from where it happened. Whether he was there and saw it I do not know, but his son, Howard, a few years older than I am, told me that he could clearly remember an occasion when, as a small boy, he was walking up Sandy Hill Road with his father, 'And,' Howard said, 'we had just walked up past the White House. You remember, where old Billy Davies the gardener used to live? And we passed a gate going into a field, it was the field where Tom Roblin used to keep his horse, and Dad said to me, 'That's the field where Bill Frost flew his aeroplane from.'

Well, yes, I said, I remembered where old Billy Davies lived, because his son married my stepmother's sister. And I remembered Tom Roblin, too, because he was one of the traditional village shopkeepers in the pre-supermarket days, for whom cargoes were delivered under sail to Saundersfoot harbour by the coastal trader, *Lady of the Isles*. His shop was on the corner, known naturally enough as Roblin's Corner, at the bottom of the hill known as High Street, and in my boyhood he was still operating his hand-turned coffee mill, and had notches on his mahogany counter for measuring an ounce of twist. He needed his horse to fetch his supplies from the harbour, once they had arrived there, and at one time to deliver round the rural areas.

Howard, as a boy, lived at Plantation Cottages, just up the road from Bill Frost. The big pal of his boyhood days was Bill Frost's grandson, Alfred, and he spent many hours playing about in and around the old man's carpenter's workshop, so he, too, became familiar with the stories that were told and their place in the history of the community.

By that time, Bill Frost's older son, Wilfred, had also become a carpenter, but worked for Fred Richards, one of the three builders in the village who spent their time tendering against each other for what little work there was to be had in those years of depression, so was in competition with my father. Even though there might not have been open hostility exactly, there was certainly no great degree of fraternisation. On the other hand, Wilfred was Secretary of the Bethany Chapel, so he was occasionally in the vicinity to drop in for a chat with his neighbour and cousin by marriage, Jack Griffiths, in his carpenter's shop alongside.

More than eighty years later I cannot claim or expect to remember word for word what was said, but always there has been that little memory of having heard the two craftsmen, one the son and the other the nephew by marriage of the man involved, as they talked of the flying machine, and what might have been done, if only so-and-so and such-and-such, by way of improvement and so on.

When Wilfred died in 1937, the *Narberth Weekly News*, in reporting on his death, said, 'Mr Frost was a son of the late Mr Wm Frost, who will always be associated with aviation, he being one of the first men to build and fly his own aeroplane.' Nobody queried such a statement nor, at that time, would anyone in Saundersfoot have thought of doing so, because they knew the story for themselves.

Another of that era with a vivid recollection of Bill Frost was the late Frankie Williams, who died in 1995 at the age of ninety-three. He, too was another from a long line of carpenters, whose three brothers all followed their father, George, at his trade, but Frankie set out in 1926 to make a future for himself in Canada, only to break his kneecap working on a farm there and come home with a stiff leg. Oddly enough he spent his last years in one of the old people's block of flats which had once been the Bethany Chapel. A couple of years before he died he went on record as saying, 'Yes, I remember Bill Frost. Clever old boy he was. I remember during the First World War when these things came over Saundersfoot. Not planes – airships these were. And the poor old man, I can see him now. He was jumping up and down and pointing. "I said they could do it. Look, look, I said they could do it." '

One member of Bill Frost's family who would almost certainly have witnessed the flight would have been his eighteen-year-old daughter, Ethel. Her daughter, Ena Mortimer, told how, when she was a child in school in Ammanford, the teacher would ask who was the first person to fly and what was the name of the inventor, and Ena would put up her hand and say, 'My grandfather, William Frost.' The teacher would say, 'No, it was the Wright brothers,' and Ena would say, 'No, Miss, it was my grandfather, William Frost.'

Another who was as likely as anybody to have witnessed the flight of Bill Frost's machine, and certainly to have known a great deal about it, was his sister, Sarah Watkins. Her daughter, Doris, was born in 1898, so that the great happening of the pioneering flight was sufficiently fresh in Sarah's mind for her to be able to tell the child with a fair degree of accuracy what had happened. Doris married Will Badham, and she it was who pointed out the oak tree, where Bill Frost crashed, to their son, and her own grandson, John Badham.

Sarah had two sons who became bakers. Fred, Josie's father, carried on the bakery business at Griffithston Hill, which had been there in the days of Bill Frost's father, and he delivered bread to us at the Bethany Manse. Born in 1893, he would have been about three years old when Bill Frost made his flight, and he it was who told of seeing part of the wreckage of the machine in the brambles when he was a boy.

There were certainly brambles there even then. Another

schoolday mate of mine, Lewis Hilling, was born and brought up at Foxenholes where his family had lived for generations, not far across the fields from Griffithston Hill and the site of the fatal landing nearer to Bethesda. Lewis said that his father, Billy Hilling, told him that his own father, another Lewis, who might well have been another to witness the event, had told him that Bill Frost had been pulling thorns out of his face for days and days after it happened. A bit of hyperbole, possibly, but it made the point, which is not intended as any sort of pun or witticism.

Of the younger generation, David Taylor, when he was a small boy, spent much time talking to his late grandfather, another William Frost, but known as Billy, founder of the Saundersfoot ironmongery business, which still goes under the name of Frosts. Billy Frost, named after his grandfather, was the son of Wilfred Frost, who, as a boy, would probably have worked with his father, Bill Frost, on building the aeroplane, and was as likely as anyone to have been there when he flew it. Billy Frost would have heard the story both from his father and grandfather, and he always stressed that Bill Frost had not been in the 'plane when it was destroyed in the storm, but that it had definitely flown before that happened. This much, of course, is the well-established gist of the story and was common knowledge, but it is interesting to hear of it as having come from someone who would most certainly have heard it many times from one who had no doubt been there as a witness to it.

The late Bobby Nash, in all probability a descendant of the family of Rebecca Nash, tells of a well-known Saundersfoot character, the late William Beddoe, a butcher who, at the time of Bill Frost's flight, grazed cattle on the field known as Steart, where part of the wreckage of Bill Frost's machine finished up after the great storm. At that time Billy Beddoe would have been about twenty-five years

William Frost's Flying Machine, drawn by a Western Mail *artist from the patent specifications*

HURRICANE NIGHT

FLYING MACHINE INVENTOR'S TRAGEDY

Special to "The People"

FORTY years ago, William Frost, a humble village carpenter, was on the verge of fame.

Though hampered by the lack of money and lack of material, he toiled and laboured until there stood before him the fruits of his inventive brain—a delicately-modelled, graceful flying machine.

William Frost was satisfied. He had faith in his machine. But that faith

THE PEOPLE, SUNDAY, OCTOBER 9, 1932

ROBBED OF FORTUNE

BY A

HURRICANE NIGHT

FLYING MACHINE INVENTOR'S TRAGEDY

The story in The People, *9 October, 1932*

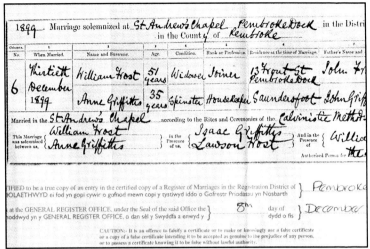

William Frost and Anne Griffiths' Marriage Certificate

William Frost and his second wife, Anne (née Griffiths)

Bill Frost (inset) at the lathe. His two sons standing next to him. Wilfred left and Lawson 2nd left.

The workmen are those of the builder B.J. Howells, the author's father, standing extreme left. Jack Griffiths (inset), standing next to him 2nd left, was his foreman carpenter.

Railway Street, Saundersfoot, c. 1900. Number 9 is halfway along on the right-hand side by the low forecourt wall – that was Bill Frost's home when the idea came to him that he could fly.

Railway Street at a later date

Saundersfoot today from Griffithston Hill.

Saundersfoot from the harbour

Cliff Cottage

Wogan Street, looking up hill from the village, with Cliff Cottage on the right towards the top.

Railway Street today. Now known as The Strand.

Welsh airman beat Wrights to the skies

by Andrew Alderson

PEMBROKESHIRE 1896

The story covered by The Sunday Times, 26.7.98.

Miss Josie Watkins showing the point of take-off (now overgrown) from Griffithston Hill side of the field at the rear of the house. The piles of ashes beneath the brambles were an accumulation over the years from Fred Watkins' (her father's) bakery.

The view from the field, with John Badham pointing to the point of take-off. Saundersfoot in the background

The author and John Badham pointing to the tree in the distance

The tree

The field showing route of flight with the tree circled.
The two electricity or telephone poles were positioned at a later date.

Griffithston Hill. The field from which Bill Frost flew was the other side of the house.

Griffithston Lane leading to the stream over which Bill Frost made the platform to build his plane

Looking over the little valley to Hopshill. It was down this valley that the wreckage of Bill Frost's plane was blown.

Storm damage in Tenby harbour on the night in 1896 when Bill Frost's plane was destroyed.

The family grave where Bill Frost was buried but without his name being inscribed on the stone.

Headstone of John Frost, Bill's father.

Headstone of Margaretta, Bill's first wife.

The author and Lewis Hilling when they had dug the fallen headstone of the Frost family out of the earth.

Headstone of Rebecca Davies, mother of Bill Frost by her first marriage. When she was widowed, she married Jeremeiah Davies.

The late Mrs Ena Mortimer at the age of eighty-seven. The last surviving grandchild of Bill Frost.

Early scenes at Saundersfoot

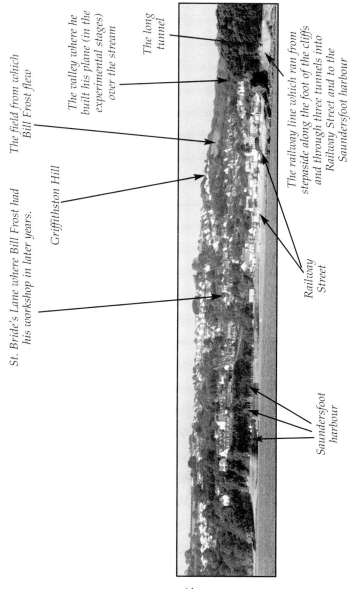

The long tunnel

The valley where he built his plane (in the experimental stages) over the stream

The field from which Bill Frost flew

The railway line which ran from stepaside along the foot of the cliffs and through three tunnels into Railway Street and to the Saundersfoot harbour

Griffithston Hill

Railway Street

St. Bride's Lane where Bill Frost had his workshop in later years.

Saundersfoot harbour

of age. As a boy, Bobby worked for him, and he remembers well how, during the Second World War, the Americans landed light aircraft on the beach at Saundersfoot, to the great surprise and excitement of the villagers, who had never seen such a thing done before, and the septuagenarian Billy Beddoe saying, 'That's nothing. And they're not the first ones to fly from Saundersfoot. Old Bill Frost did that years ago.'

His brother, Frank Beddoe, who deserted the family's long tradition of butchering to become yet another carpenter, worked occasionally with my father, and I can still vaguely remember conversations between him and Jack Griffiths, in the old carpenter's shop, about Bill Frost and his aeroplane, on the same lines as the many similar discussions between Jack Griffiths and Bill Frost's son, Wilfred.

When Bill Frost died in March, 1935, the *Tenby Observer* reported his death under the headlines:

'Saundersfoot Man Who Built An
Aeroplane Forty Years Ago
Death Of The Grand Old Man Of Aviation In Wales
Remarkable Story Of Wm. Frost's
Early Experiments

A career crowded with interest and ambition has been brought to a close by the death, which occurred on Friday last, of Mr W. Frost, of St Bride's Lane, Saundersfoot.

Mr Frost, who was 87 years of age, had spent the greater part of his life in his native Saundersfoot, and he could claim to have been one of the pioneers of aircraft design. Half a century ago he was convinced that air transport was a practical proposition, and he designed, patented and built an aeroplane which was the first to be constructed in Britain.

At the time representatives from several foreign countries

65

came to Saundersfoot to interview Mr Frost and to endeavour to buy his patent. One offer, which was made by a German Representative, would have made him a wealthy man had he accepted, but he turned them all down in the hope that one day, when the plane was perfected to his satisfaction, he could offer the patent to his own government.

Mr Frost, who had been blind for many years, died at the home of his daughter at Penybanc, Ammanford. His wife predeceased him about six months ago.'

If not entirely accurate in one or two respects, which can be considered later, the headline comes fairly near to dating the flight insofar as it says 'forty years ago'. This was a nice round figure, whereas thirty-nine would have been more accurate.

It must be significant, however, even to the doubters, that such a banner headline appeared in a local paper all that time ago and so soon after the epic flight, within the living memory of so many still living in the village. It tells us what we already know, and that is that the story at that time was fully known to the people of the area, and nobody would have queried it. There was no question of if, or but, or maybe. Bill Frost had built and flown an aeroplane and that was all there was to it.

The other interesting reference was to the fact that he had died in Ammanford at the home of his daughter. That was the second Ethel, named after the first baby of that name, who had died when she was a month old.

For whatever reason, there was no follow-up or even a report of the funeral, and now the event has long since passed into history and been virtually forgotten. By the time interest was rekindled more recently, there was not even any recollection locally as to where he had been buried. One descendant, now deceased, admittedly not all that reliable, assured me that it had been in St Issell's churchyard, and that he distinctly remembered seeing the gravestone, which struck me as odd for such a staunch nonconformist, when there was a graveyard at Bethesda, where he had married Margaretta, and where she and two of their children, as well as his mother, had been buried. It was also the sister chapel to his beloved Bethany. Then, so it was said, he had indeed been buried at Bethesda in the same grave as Margaretta and their two daughters, but there was no evidence of this. All that had been visible as far as most people could seem to remember was what looked like the base of a headstone, with the names, ages and dates of the deaths of Margaretta and the two girls. Bill Frost would no doubt have seen to that at the time, before his own time came more than forty-odd years later.

Lewis Hilling's wife, Hettie, however, the Secretary to Bethesda Chapel, produced the note-book with the hand-written entry which tells us that Bill Frost was indeed buried there in 1935. Lewis was able to go one better and say that, before the more recent interest, he seemed to remember, a long time ago, having seen a cross lying on the ground alongside the plinth. So we went there, armed with a spade, called on Mel Davies, a capable photographer and an old friend, but not as old as we are, living nearby, and they removed much soil and decaying grass and dug up the cross for Mel to take a few pictures.

There was no name on it. By the time Bill Frost, blind and a virtual pauper, had joined his loved ones in their last long sleep, or gone on to join them in a richer, fuller living, according to which way you care to consider such matters, there was no money left in that era of economic depression to record his own name. But most certainly he has not been, nor ever can be, forgotten.

Chapter 7

What The Papers Said

Apart from the brief newspaper references to Bill Frost already quoted, there are, as far as is known, only two others of any substance. They are worth examining in some detail because, apart from any other considerations, they give us a rather better idea and understanding as to where Bill Frost, a working man with few resources of his own, and no financial backing whatsoever, built his flying machine.

There has been an idea recently that he would have built it in his little carpenter's shop, a converted cottage alongside his home near the top of St Bride's Lane. Such a suggestion can be immediately discounted when we remember the dimensions of the machine, as we now know them to have been. Even more relevant is the knowledge that Bill Frost did not marry Annie Griffiths of Stammers Cottage until three years after the tragic end to his flight.

The first of the two significant newspaper reports appeared in the *Western Mail* on September 29th, 1932, under the by-line, H.G. Walters. A native of Pembrokeshire, Glyn Walters was at that time a reporter on the *Western Mail*. Shortly afterwards he acquired the local papers, the *Narberth Weekly News* and its sister paper, the *Tenby*

Observer. When he reported the death of 'The Grand Old Man Of Aviation In Wales' in those papers in 1935, he was, therefore, as Editor, able to quote from his own report of 1932, which is worth reading again in its entirety:

'WELSH PIONEER OF AIRCRAFT DESIGN
Modern Device that was Invented 40 Years ago

Famous flying experts who have visited Wales at different times have rebuked us as a nation for lagging behind in the development of air travel. They tell us we have been content just to follow in the wake of aeronautical progress.

Perhaps they are not aware that forty years ago, before most of the present-day world flyers and speed record-breakers were born, before any man had risen above the earth in a mechanically propelled machine, a Welshman actually built and patented a "flying machine" that embodied the principles of the gyroscope, which is now regarded as the last word in modern aircraft design.

The inventor, a modest Pembrokeshire carpenter, was doomed to failure by lack of funds; by the sceptical attitude of the complacent England of forty years ago, when any suggestion of conquering the highways of the air was merely ridiculed as fantastic. And, as though Fate was conspiring against him, a sudden storm one night wrecked the strange craft that had taken him a few years to build, and with which he hoped to prove to an unbelieving world that air-travel was a practical proposition.

The Pioneer's Dreams

But the specifications of that ill-fated flying machine are still reposing in the musty archives of H.M. Patent Office as permanent proof that Wales has had its pioneers in the realms of aviation.

A few weeks ago I had the good fortune to meet the veteran inventor and to secure a copy of the patent papers relating to his remarkable craft.

I found William Frost sitting beside an old-fashioned chimney-place in his cottage, which is almost hidden from view by a profusion of lilac trees on the hillside overlooking the peaceful bay of Saundersfoot.

He is now 84 and he spends the gloaming of a life of hard struggle to dreaming over again the dreams of forty years ago.

Bill Frost, as he is known to the village, cannot see the holiday planes that frequently pass over the bay to and from Tenby, or the powerful Air Force machines from Pembroke Dock, for his eyes are dimmed with age. But sometimes he hears the roar of an engine overhead and just nods his head knowingly, and a wistful smile passes over his face.

He is not embittered because success and affluence eluded him; he is, in fact, intensely proud that his ideas have proved practical, though others have received the honours.

An Old Man's Story

When the old fellow told me the story of his flying machine he chuckled when he related how it was found one morning half-a-dozen fields away, a mass of twisted wreckage.

"Anyways, if that gale hadn't a sprung up I should not a' bin here now to tell you the story," he philosophised in the musical dialect of his county. Then he went on to tell me how the idea of flying first occurred to him. He was still in his 'teens' and working at his trade at Hean Castle, the Pembrokeshire residence of Lord Merthyr.

One wintry afternoon, when a strong sou'westerly wind was blowing, young Frost was carrying a large plank of light timber on his shoulders. A sudden gust caught the plank at the most effective angle until it lifted the lad completely off his feet for a second or two. With that gust of wind was born the first dream of wings that would ride through the air.

It was some years later before Frost commenced to put his schemes to the test. The problem before him was twofold: to raise the machine off the ground, and then to induce its motion through the air. The machine, therefore, became something of a "cross" between the airship and the glider. Petrol engines were then unknown.

Frost had built and patented his flying machine a dozen years before the late M. Alberte Santos-Dumont, the world-famous aeronautical inventor, achieved the first fluttering hopes from the ground in a power-driven machine in August 1906, and fifteen years before an authentic flight in a man-carrying aeroplane equipped with an engine was made by Orville Wright at Dayton, Ohio.

One-man Power

According to the specifications of Frost's machine it consisted of two cigar-like chambers, one above the other, constructed of wirework and covered with light waterproof material. The upper chamber was filled with hydrogen gas sufficient to lift the machine without its pilot.

In the lower compartment the pilot was seated, and it was in order to provide the extra lifting power to raise both machine and passenger that Frost adopted the gyroscope principle. Above the upper chamber was a propeller – or what the inventor described as a "vertical fan".

It was attached to a steel shaft running down through

the gas-chamber to the pilot's compartment. Here it was operated by the pilot by means of a bevelled friction gearing device, so that the pilot was able to wind the propeller until it attained sufficient force to raise the machine into the air.

There were two wings, one on either side of the gas-chamber, and when a certain height had been attained the pilot would stop the hand-driven propeller. It was then that the gliding motion would become effective. The machine would travel downwards and onwards until momentum had been gained. It was directed upwards again by a tail rudder worked by wires from the pilot's compartment, the upwards gradient being also aided by the hand-driven propeller. While the tail rudder directed the upward and downward motion, a similar device on the front of the machine controlled its sideways direction.

Just as the gyroscope propeller served to raise the craft, so it enabled the pilot to regulate a gentle landing.

A War Secretary's Reply

Crude and grotesque as it all may seem to this scientific age, William Frost's flying machine might well have accomplished the world's first aeroplane flight had not fate struck its cruel blow and shattered his best laid plans.

Afterwards work took him to London and family responsibilities handicapped him, financially and otherwise, in any further endeavour.

His patent was accepted on October 19th, 1896, and, still full of confidence in the possibilities of his invention, he later sent the plans and specifications of his machine to the Secretary of State for War.

The reply he received, written by Mr St John Brodrick, the Under-Secretary of State for the War Department, is rather amusing in these days. In thanking Frost for allowing him to peruse the papers, Mr Brodrick wrote: "The nation does not intend to adopt aerial navigation as a means of warfare."!

But William Frost has lived to see the new world he dreamt of 40 years ago. It is little wonder that he enjoys recalling those dreams as he sits in his old-fashioned chimney-place waiting for the final flight.'

Before looking more closely at this little piece of history it would perhaps be as well to turn to the other report first, and then examine the two together. It appeared in *The People*, shortly afterwards, on Sunday, October 9th, 1932:

'ROBBED OF FORTUNE
BY A
HURRICANE
NIGHT
FLYING MACHINE
INVENTOR'S
TRAGEDY
Special To the "People"

Forty years ago, William Frost, a humble village carpenter, was on the verge of fame.

Though hampered by the lack of money and the lack of material, he toiled and laboured until there stood before him the fruits of his inventive brain – a delicately modelled, graceful flying machine.

William Frost was satisfied. He had faith in his machine. But that faith was never to be put to the test. Before the flying machine took to the air it was wrecked in a gale.

Today at the age of eighty-five, blind and poor, Frost sits in his little cottage at Saundersfoot, ten miles from Pembroke Dock, thinking wistfully of the great days he might have had.

The occasional roar of a 'plane overhead may comfort

him; the noise of the engine is proof that his dreams of the conquest of the air were not in vain.

Worked Alone

The old man told me the story of his wrecked hopes and ambitions, as he sat looking with unseeing eyes towards the autumn sunshine.

His machine was 25ft long and built of bamboo covered with thin canvas.

There were two wings, one on either side of the gas chamber, and a hand-driven propeller was devised to give a forward motion. Above the gas chamber were two vertical fans in order to provide the extra lifting power to raise both machine and passenger. Another compartment 15ft long was adapted to carry the inventor.

"Building the machine was an anxious business, but I have the satisfaction of knowing that I am the inventor of air travel.

"I put some girders across a stream, placed on them a floor of wood, and there I saw the creature of my brain come slowly into being.

"I could ask no one for advice, I had no books to refer to. But I was the first man to construct a flying machine, and I walked alone.

"A man who heard of me came down to see me from London. He was a son of the famous Jenny Lind, and rode the whole way on horseback. I told him I had gone practically as far as I could go; it was more money I wanted.

'But I was afraid that if I could not pay him back he would claim my machine and patent. Perhaps I was green, who knows?

"*My machine was finished. It was a night in September – a peaceful night, but there was no peace in my breast. It was going to fly, I was going to rival the birds in their element, my name was going to be handed down as a man who built with his own hands the first ship of the sky.*

"I went to bed and was awakened by the roar of the wind, the crash of the breakers on the shore of the bay, and I feared for the safety of the machine. When it was light I went down to see how it had fared and found it scattered about a field some distance away."

With a catch in his voice the old man continued: 'Mine was a heavy heart. My dream was shattered; my toil in vain.

"I went to London to work. I was bent on saving enough money to start again. I worked hard, but could not save it, so my patent lapsed. Others saw the specifications of my machine, and picked my brains.

Money does not bring happiness, but a lack of it shattered my hopes." '

I left William Frost, a pioneer of air travel, alone with his memories.

There are, as would be expected, certain discrepancies between the two reports, and in some cases obvious inaccuracies in the reports themselves, but they do indeed shed valuable light on some of what is already known.

The style of *The People* article can be discounted. Anyone with an ounce of common sense will recognise immediately that they are not listening to Bill Frost talking, or more correctly perhaps, making such a speech. In places it made him sound more like a boastful man of arrogance than the modest village carpenter. He must have squirmed with embarrassment at the hyperbole, if not downright literary slush, when the paper appeared and somebody would have read it to him. He would have told his story, and words would have been put into his mouth.

There is the thought, too, that the report in the *People* was headed:

Special To the 'People'

There was no by-line, so we cannot discount the strong possibility that the special correspondent would in fact have been Glyn Walters. On the staff of the *Western Mail*, his identity would not have been disclosed by the *People*, and it was common practice anyway for a staff reporter to be on the lookout for picking up a bit extra here-and-there whenever the chance offered. And Glyn was ever well-known for 'wanting the bean for the pea', as they say in Pembrokeshire, when he eventually became a newspaper proprietor himself.

In fairness to Glyn, however, whilst deploring the style of the report in the *People*, if he had indeed written it, his own report as submitted would no doubt have been mangled considerably, as will be readily appreciated by those who have suffered from seeing their own work subjected to the treatment.

Apart from one brief effort, Glyn Walters, in his story in the *Western Mail*, avoided the alleged direct quote, which was fortunate. He could not write in the Pembrokeshire dialect, because he could not speak it. And he could not speak it because, although a native of the county, he was not from 'down below', as we call it, but from north of the so-called non-existent Landsker, that imaginary divide which runs from Amroth in the far south-east corner, or possibly from the mouth of the river Taf, slightly further to the east, to Newgale in the north-west.

The son of a nonconformist minister, however, he was very much in tune spiritually with Bill Frost, as he showed in his delightful conclusion to his report of the interview where he wrote, 'It is little wonder that he enjoys recalling those dreams as he sits in his old-fashioned chimney-place waiting for the final flight.'

With the solitary interview, as distinct from the carefully researched piece, there is always the danger of certain inaccuracies, and Glyn Walters was well off-beam with his references to the dates and doings of the other well-known pioneers of aviation, but he was almost exactly right when he referred to the dreams of forty years previously, even though he was slightly out with the exact date when the patent was registered. And we have already referred to the exact date, and therefore Bill Frost's age, when Hean Castle was rebuilt.

Note, too, that the one report was of a machine that was strange, crude and grotesque, whilst the other referred to the same machine as graceful.

To those who know the area, it will be of interest to read of the aeroplanes flying to and from Tenby. There never was anything faintly resembling an airfield at or near Tenby, but the report appeared at a time when pleasure flights were being run from the town's expansive South beach. The famous Sunderland flying-boats had also just come to the great waterway at Pembroke Dock.

All this apart, the real value of these two separate reports is that they establish beyond any reasonable doubt where Bill Frost built his flying machine. Even a journalist with the most vivid imagination and colourful turn of phrase could not have dreamed up the idea of Bill Frost 'putting two iron girders across a stream and building a wooden platform on top of them'.

The stream, as will be immediately recognised by those who know the area, was the one which runs close to where the cottages were at the foot of Griffithston Hill, with a ford near the cottage known as Long Park, so close to where Bill Frost was living with his mother at the time. That stream eventually runs down through the valley close to where the Beddoes had their slaughterhouse at what was known as

Beddoe's Yard. The stream was known as Beddoe's Lake, and still is to those of an older generation. The term lake, or *laak*, was well established in the Pembrokeshire dialect as being applied to running water. A gentleman from the Home Counties, who had lived in Saundersfoot all of fifteen years at the time, told me fairly recently that fifty years or so ago there had been a lake there and there were boats on it. I expressed interest and thanked him for the helpful information.

Not needing too much by way of a geography or history lesson on the subject of Beddoe's Lake, neither did I need to read a newspaper report as to where Bill Frost had built his 'plane in the experimental stages. That bit of knowledge came to me early in life, and the year was 1929, on April 27th, on the occasion of the F.A. Cup Final at Wembley, exactly six months before my tenth birthday.

The little seaside village, as it then was, of Saundersfoot, in those days of depression, had a football team which was the best in the whole County, and one of the few things about which we could cheer. We village boys were fervent supporters and football-mad. Everybody likes to follow a winning team. Young Billy Frost, grandson of Bill Frost after whom he had been named, and whose father, Wilfred, son of the old man, had worked with him on his 'plane, had just acquired a wireless and was not averse to showing it off. They lived in one of the cottages halfway down, on the left-hand side, of what was then known as Griffithston Lane, and a few of us boys living nearby were welcome to listen.

'When two are stripped, long ere the course begin, we wish that one should lose the other win.'

That Cup Final was between Bolton and Portsmouth, and I wanted Portsmouth to win, for no better reason than the fact that Billy Weddle played for them. He was a 'left-footer', and so was I. In those cigarette card days his picture was on one of them, fair-haired and handsome. My fourteen-year-old sister was the one who said how handsome he was, apart from the fact that we had an uncle and cousins living in Portsmouth, so those were two more good reason for wanting them to win, but Bolton beat them two-nil. We remember so many of these unrelated happenings as the years go by, and that is why I can name the date when I learned where Bill Frost built his 'plane.

There was a man there that day, of whom I have no recollection whatsoever, except that he and Wilfred were talking about the girders and the platform over the stream, which was maybe a hundred yards or so a bit further along at the end of the lane. It meant nothing to me that day, especially when there was something far more important, such as the F.A. Cup Final, to occupy a small boy's mind. But it meant that when the time came many years later for people to talk about it, I knew where Bill Frost had built his 'plane.

Piece by patient piece he would have built his machine, and then, when he was ready, assembled it on his platform. Once satisfied that he had it right, he would have dismantled it and carted the various components up to the top of the field from which he intended to fly.

Then we come to the reference to his saying that, after the storm, he found the parts half-a-dozen fields away. That field, as we know, was Steart. And Steart, where in the benign Pembrokeshire climate the Beddoe's cattle would no doubt have been grazing an ample bite of latter grass, was all of half-a-dozen fields away from the oak tree where he had come to grief.

Then, again, he said that, after the storm, he 'went down' the next morning. It would be all too easy to assume that he meant that he went down to the platform. A Saundersfoot man talks of up-off, up to London, or up-line, especially since the railway came, or up to anywhere to the east. Likewise, he will speak of going down to Pembroke or anywhere to the west. And that historic oak tree was due west exactly.

So we come to the very significant statement that his faith was never put to the test, and the thought that there was no reference to the flight or to the oak tree. His 'plane had been put to the test and flown for something like five hundred yards before the crash, but there had been no chance to salvage the wreckage and rebuild it to fly again with the world there to watch.

Bill Frost was an old man, dreaming his dreams. In his time he would no doubt have been the subject of much good-natured leg-pulling to his face perhaps, but undoubtedly of even more ridicule and unkind words behind his back, and, in the close-knit community of that small village, he would most certainly have been aware of it. He would have experienced much of that whilst he was carrying out his tests and working on his plans, and by the time of his flight he would probably have wanted as few people there as possible. He would have been by no means unusual in that respect. The history of all those who were making similar plans and attempts at that time are reputed to have been secretive beyond words in all that they did.

Certainly, nearly half-a-century later, he would have been cautious in speaking to the two strangers, or possibly it could have been just the one stranger, who would be reporting to the world what he was saying. He would have been content to dream his dreams, and, whilst prepared to tell something of the true story to those he knew, the last thing he would have wanted to admit to outsiders was that his venture, as far as the world was concerned, had ended in failure.

There is, too, the fact that by this time the important question concerning those who were now enquiring would have been to establish whether Bill Frost really did fly at all, and not anything specific about the exact point of departure or the exact route he took or tried to take, or what he meant exactly by 'went down'. As the years went by it would have been all too easy for those who were not familiar with the exact details to assume that he would have headed straight out across the valley.

Although there is no record of his having said so himself, even if some of the wreckage was indeed found in Steart, that would almost certainly have been the canvas and lighter materials. The reports of the damage elsewhere during that horrendous storm call for no stretch of the imagination to visualise such material being whisked away and leaving the heavier metal parts under the tree.

Chapter 8

Bill Frost's Flying Machine

Having come so far with the story of Bill Frost himself it would perhaps be as well at this stage to say something more about his machine as far as can be ascertained from his patent.

We saw earlier something of Bill Frost's provisional application, and now we come to the greater detail and the acceptance of his patent.

'Victoria By the Grace of God Of the United Kingdom of Great Britain and Ireland, Queen, Defender of the faith: To all to whom these presents shall come,

Greeting:
    Whereas William Frost Carpenter and Builder
    Saundersfoot Pembrokeshire . . .
hath presented unto us that he is in possession of an invention for . . . a flying machine . . . that he is the true and first inventor thereof, and that the same is not in use by any other person, to the best of his knowledge and belief:

AND WHEREAS the said inventor hath humbly prayed that We would be graciously pleased to grant unto him (hereinafter, together with his executors, administrators, and assigns, or any of them, referred to as the said patentee)

our Royal Letters Patent for the sole use and advantage of his said invention:

AND WHEREAS the said inventor hath by and in his complete specification particularly described the nature of his said invention:

AND WHEREAS We, being willing to encourage all inventions which may be for the public good are graciously pleased to condescend to his request:

KNOW YE, THEREFORE, that We of our especial grace, certain knowledge and mere motion, do by these presents, for us, our heirs and successors, give and grant unto the said patentee our especial licence, full power, sole privilege, and authority that the said patentee, by himself, his agents, or licensees, and no others, may at all times hereafter, during the term of years herein mentioned, make, use, exercise, and vend the said invention within the United Kingdom of Great Britain and Ireland and Isle of Man in such manner as to him or them seem meet, and that the said patentee shall have and enjoy the whole profit and advantage from time to time accruing by reason of the said invention during the term of fourteen years from the date hereunder written of these presents: AND to the end that the said patentee may have and enjoy the sole use and exercise, and the full benefit of the said invention, We do by these presents, for us, our heirs and successors, strictly command all our subjects whatsoever, within our United Kingdom of Great Britain and Ireland and the Isle of Man, that they do not at any time during the said term of fourteen years either directly or indirectly, make use of, or put in practice the said invention, or any part of the same, nor in anywise imitate the same, nor make, or cause to be made, any addition thereto or subtraction therefrom, whereby to pretend themselves the inventors thereof, without the consent, license, or agreement of the said patentee in writing under his hand and seal, on pain of incurring such penalties as may be justly inflicted on such offenders for their contempt of this our Royal command, and of being answerable to the patentee according to law for his damages occasioned:

PROVIDED that these our letters patent are on this condition: that if at any time during the said term it be made to appear to us, our heirs or successors, or any six or more of our Privy Council that this our grant is contrary to law, or prejudicial or inconvenient to our subjects in general, or that the said invention is not a new invention as to the public use and exercise thereof within our United Kingdom of Great Britain and Ireland and Isle of Man, or that the said patentee is not the first and true inventor thereof within this realm as aforesaid, these our letters patent shall forthwith determine, and be void to all intents and purposes, not withstanding anything herein before contained: PROVIDED ALSO, that if the said patentee shall not pay all fees by law required to be paid in respect of the grant of these letters patent, or in respect of any matter relating thereto, at the time or times and in manner for the time being by law provided; and also if the said patentee shall not supply, or cause to be supplied, for our service all such articles of the said invention as may be required by the officers or commissioners administering any department of our service, in such manner, at such times, and at and upon such reasonable prices and terms as shall be settled in manner for the time being by law provided, then, and in any of the said cases, these our letters patent, and all privileges and advantages whatever hereby granted, shall determine and become void, not withstanding anything herein before contained: PROVIDED ALSO, that nothing herein contained shall prevent the granting of licenses in such manner and for such considerations as they may by law be granted: AND lastly, we do by these presents, for us, our heirs and successors, grant unto the said patentee that these our letters patent shall be construed in the most beneficial sense for the advantage of the said patentee.

IN WITNESS whereof we have caused these our letters to be made patent this twenty fifth day of October one thousand eight hundred and ninety four and to be sealed as of the twenty fifth day of October one thousand eight hundred and ninety four.

H. READER LACK

Comptroller-General of Patents.'

'COMPLETE SPECIFICATION

A Flying Machine

William Frost Builder Saundersfoot Pembrokeshire do hereby declare the nature of this invention and in what manner the same is to be performed, to be particularly described and ascertained in and by the following statement:

The flying machine is constructed with an upper and lower chamber of wire work covered with light waterproof material. Each chamber formed sharp at both ends with parallel side. The upper large chamber to contain sufficient gas to lift the machine. In the centre of upper chamber a cylinder is fixed in which a horizontal fan is driven by means of a shaft and bevelled gearing worked from the lower chamber. When the machine has been risen to a sufficient height, then the fan is stopped and the upper chamber which has wings attached is tilted forward causing the machine to move, as a bird onward and downward. When low enough it is again tilted in an opposite direction which causes it to soar upward and onward when it is again assisted if necessary by the fan. The steering is done by a rudder at both ends.

The flying machine is constructed with an upper and lower chamber of wire work covered with light waterproof material. Each chamber formed sharp at both ends with parallel sides. The upper chamber as shown on drawings at B to contain sufficient gas to lift the machine. In the centre of upper chamber B a cylinder is fixed in which a horizontal fan as shown at A is driven by means of a shaft as shown at H and bevelled gearing as shown at G worked from the lower chamber – as shown at K.

When the machine has risen to a sufficient height, then the fan A is stopped and the upper chamber B which has wings attached is tilted forward, by lines as shown at E causing the machine to move as a bird onward and downward. When low enough it is again tilted in an opposite direction which causes it to soar upward and onward, when it is again assisted by the fan A if necessary.

The steering is done by a rudder at both ends as shown at C and D.

Having now particularly described and ascertained the nature of my said invention and in what manner the same is to be performed, I declare that what I claim is:

1. The separate motive powers, namely the gas for lifting the machine only and the horizontal fan or regulator as shown at A which lifts those who are in the machine, and when reversed it assists the down motion or weight on the wings.

2. The tilting of the upper chamber & wings as shown at B which causes the machine to move onward and downward, and when the tilting is reversed it moves & upward. This is done by wire lines as shown at E passing over a wheel as shown at F and turned either as required.

3. The working of the horizontal fan in the cylinder as shown at A. This is done by two driving wheels as shown at

G with bevelled friction gearing fixed to a shaft as shown at H and turns the fan. The driving wheels are fixed on a suspended frame I which keeps the shaft H in a straight position when the tilting takes place.

4. The steering which is done by a rudder as shown at C fixed on front end of upper chamber in a vertical position and is moved either way by lines as shown at J and worked from lower chamber. A tail is fixed on the hinder end to assist the steering & tilting as shown at D.

5. The passenger or lower chamber as shown at K is protected from the source of the atmosphere with wire work & waterproof covering with suitable ventilation & lights.

Dated this 30th day of August 1895.

WILLIAM FROST.'

Paul Williams, to whom I am indebted for locating the exact dates of the reports in the *Western Mail* and *The People*, points out that in *The People* article there is a reference to a hand-driven propeller for forward motion, which is not shown in the Patent drawing, and he wonders whether the reporter made a mistake or whether Bill Frost subsequently modified his design. *(See drawing on page 112.)*

There is also the interesting reference to the use of bamboo, and although this was not mentioned in the plans submitted to the Patent Office, there would have been plenty of it growing in the grounds of the gentry, who would have been more than happy to make abundant supplies of it available to someone whom they probably regarded as an amiable eccentric.

One other thought is that the more technically minded have remarked on the similarity between Bill Frost's design and the helicopter, in which case he was nearer to having been fifty years ahead of his time rather than a mere seven.

Chapter 9

The Years Of Disillusionment

Having dealt with such details of the flight as are available, we come to the events which followed, and precious little is there to be found anywhere on record by way of anything relating to them.

We have seen the reference to various outside interests and foreign powers, and to the response from Mr St John Brodrick. I know that letter existed because I remember, when I was a boy, Bill Frost showing it to my father. There were other letters, too, but, after all these years, and having been only a boy at the time, I could not say now what they were. Certainly there has been a well-told story in the Frost family over the years of an offer from a German firm, which Bill Frost steadfastly refused to accept, and that, when his patent eventually lapsed, they took it up for nothing. Those who could have authenticated that story are no longer with us.

There is also the more specific reference in *The People* to the son of Jenny Lind. Paul Williams, who has done some interesting research on the Bill Frost story, points out that Jenny Lind married Otto Goldschmitt, but he was unable to trace any of their children. He even tried, without success, to trace any French or German Government offers to Bill

Frost through their Official Records in Paris and Berlin, when it was still in East Germany.

The loss, or in some cases the wilful destruction, of the various letters and papers can be dealt with later, but it is necessary to deal with as much, or as little, as has been told and handed down if the story is ever to be pieced together, and any understanding reached, of how Bill Frost's brave effort was destined to come to nothing.

After years of sacrifice, and no doubt costly trial and error, he finally built and flew his machine, as we have seen, in 1896. It is well to spell out that date again, because, looking back from the affluence of today, it is all too easy to forget that the era when Bill Frost was active has become known to history as 'The Hungry Nineties'. Is it not, therefore, somewhat illogical for sceptics to argue that, if he had really met with the success which has now been claimed for him, he would have started enthusiastically all over again after that autumn storm had destroyed his life's work? It was a time when the ordinary working man had as much as ever he could do merely to keep body and soul together.

It is not only from what appeared in the two newspapers in the 1930's that we know he went away to London to try to earn enough money to keep his patent in being and perhaps start again.

It will be remembered that, when the application for his patent was acknowledged, it stated *that the said patentee shall have and enjoy the whole profit and advantage from time to time accruing by reason of the said invention during the term of fourteen years from the date hereunder written of these presents:*

That was dated the twenty-fifth day of October, 1894, so that his patent would have lapsed in 1908. The fee to register it in the first place had been £1-0-0 on filing the provisional specification, and another £4-0-0 on filing the complete specification. There was then a further charge of £1-0-0 for 'sealing' the patent prior to grant, and figures were attached to show what it would have cost to renew it and keep it in being for the full term of fourteen years, and there is no need to ask why a poor village carpenter, having staked his all, would have had not the remotest realistic hope of renewing it for very long, if at all. The cost of the Patent Form itself had just gone up from eightpence (proper money as distinct from the post-decimalised Mickey Mouse variety) to one shilling, so that the significance of the word inflation, even so long ago, had already reared its ugly head. Amongst the pitifully few documents belonging to Bill Frost to have been discovered recently, is a covering letter written to him when the application had finally been made and had been accepted for the registration of the complete specification. It was this letter which detailed the scale of charges for renewing the patent during the fourteen years of its existence.

The letter, from the Comptroller-General, dated December 31st, 1895, simply says: 'SIR,

With reference to your Application, numbered as above, I beg to forward herewith the Patent for your Invention.

Your attention is particularly called to the note printed on the back of the Patent in reference to the payment of fees as they may become due.

I am, Sir,

Your obedient Servant
H. Reader Lack
Comptroller-General'

On the back the document states as follows:

'NOTE. – The continuance of this Patent is conditional on the payment (by way of the prescribed Patent Form J) of the following fees: £ s d

Before the expiration of the 4th year from the date of the patent }
                                and in respect of the 5th year}   5 0 0
     "   "   5th   "   6th   "   6 0 0
     "   "   6th   "   7th   "   7 0 0
     "   "   7th   "   8th   "   8 0 0
     "   "   8th   "   9th   "   9 0 0
     "   "   9th   "   10th   "   10 0 0
     "   "   10th   "   11th   "   11 0 0
     "   "   11th   "   12th   "   12 0 0
     "   "   12th   "   13th   "   13 0 0
     "   "   13th   "   14th   "   14 0 0

As the payment of these renewal fees is regulated by Act of Parliament, a fee cannot be received a *single day* after it is due; but if by accident, mistake, or inadvertence the payment has been omitted, application may be made to the Comptroller, on Patent Form 'K', for an extension of time to make such payment, specifying the reason for such omission, and for this extension the fees payable are £1 for one month, £3 for two months, or £5 for three months, but no further extension can be allowed beyond three months.'

In the absence of any definitely recorded figures or information it was always difficult to know whether Bill Frost had in fact ever raised enough money to renew his patent even once, let alone think of trying to rebuild his machine. Over the years it has generally been understood that the venture had broken him financially. In that poverty-stricken age, especially for a poor, working man who had spent every spare penny he had ever possessed on the brave, crazy venture, it seemed inconceivable that there could ever have been the faintest hope of his finding even more money to put down merely to keep a dream in being. The idea generally, even amongst some of the family who reckoned they knew something of the story, has invariably been that he went on paying every year to renew the patent until he could afford to do so no longer. For my own part, from everything I had ever been told, and the more I tried to research the background to it all, the more I became convinced that the initial payments totalling £6 would have been as much as he would ever have managed. From the reading of these documents it is evident that he would have become liable for his first renewal payment of £4 in the autumn of 1898. Then we find eventually in the *Illustrated Official Journal* (Patents) No: 527, of Wednesday, February 8th, 1899, under 'Recorded Patents void through non payment of renewal fees', the plain, heart-breaking statement, '1894-20431 Frost.'

Whatever must have been the cost of all the materials he had needed for the building of the machine, and they must have been considerable, with a measure of trial and error thrown in, the cold figure of £6 for the registration of the Patent in the last decade of the 19th Century speaks for itself. In today's money, a hundred years later, that would have to represent a figure of somewhere well in excess of a thousand pounds. And Bill Frost, a widower, who had struggled to bring up his family in days of such penury, knew nothing of Unemployment Benefit or Social Security.

When he went to London is not known exactly, but it was evidently soon after his initial bitter disappointment in 1896. Probably his younger son, Lawson, went with him, and certainly his daughter, the teenaged Ethel, did so. Child though she had been when their mother died, in 1888, she had taken her place to care for her younger brother, and she earned something for the family whilst they were in London by giving piano lessons. Like her father, she was musical, as indeed have been so many of the family down through the years. And it was in London that she met her future husband, Thomas Cale, from North Wales, who was but one of the many from the depressed rural areas to have gone to London to seek a living. They eventually married at Merthyr in 1904, before moving to Ammanford, where Tom Cale worked as a miner. They had nine children and reared six of them. One of them, Ena Mortimer, who died at ninety-three years of age, was the last surviving grandchild of Bill Frost.

Having failed in his endeavours to earn any sort of worthwhile money in London, Bill Frost had returned shortly afterwards to his native Saundersfoot. For a time he worked at his trade in the shipbuilding yard at Pembroke Dock, where, since he had no home of his own, he had been in lodgings at 13 Front Street, and it was there, on December 30th, 1899, when he was a fifty-one year old widower, that he married the thirty-five year old spinster, Annie Griffiths, at St Andrew's Calvinistic Methodist Chapel, with Annie's brother, Isaac, and young Lawson as witnesses. Annie's mother had died at Stammers Cottage two years earlier, and Bill Frost moved into Annie's home, where he was to spend the rest of his days, until he went to the home of his daughter, Ethel, at Penybanc, for the last weeks of his life before he died there in 1935.

From all that is known and remembered of him in the years following his return from London, and of that which was written from time to time of his contribution to the life of the community, he would seem to have been sufficiently resilient through it all to have accepted his failure and to have taken a good heart to life. He had his music and his chapel, and, following his days at Pembroke Dock shipyard, he had his work as a highly skilled carpenter in the workshop in the converted cottage near the top of St Bride's Lane.

At what period exactly he would have received the various offers for his patent we do not know, and now it is unlikely that we ever shall. He came to know what poverty was in the depressed years of the early 1930's, and he had his share of sorrow and family troubles, as most families do, which is yet to tell. Blind in his last years, he was regularly to be met with, as some can still recall, as he led his goats for a walk or, as someone said, maybe they led him.

Doubtless, with his greatest disappointment put behind him, he would not have wanted to open old wounds in those last years by talking too much about them to strangers.

Chapter 10

What Happened To The Papers And Why The Long Silence?

So we come to what is perhaps the most difficult chapter of all to write, not because of any absence of material or lack of facts, but because of not knowing how much to include and how much to leave out. Gossip writers and those who write of such village happenings for television plays or serials would have no shortage of material whatsoever. Perhaps that is an understatement. They would almost certainly regard it as a real bonanza, or meat and drink, or whatever the appropriate epithet might be. Dylan Thomas has gone down to posterity with his *Under Milk Wood* based on far less fertile material by drawing on the lives and antics of the good people of Laugharne, law-abiding and God-fearing. It is the only way to understand why such priceless letters could ever have been destroyed.

On the opposite side of St Bride's Lane to Stammers Cottage and Bill Frost's workshop there were a couple of adjoining cottages known as Tennyson House, where there lived, with his invalid wife and their four daughters, one Alfred Henry Lewis, known as Affie Bob. From Tenby he was, where, after the custom of that seaside town, they had sobriquets for so many of their families, especially those of the artisan class. Why 'Bob' in this particular case is not immediately clear, and irrelevant to the telling of the story of Bill Frost. It should come as a surprise to no one who has read thus far to learn that Affie Bob was a carpenter. Maybe not a particularly good carpenter as carpenters go, or as he might have been judged in the illustrious company of some of those already mentioned, but a carpenter.

He had learned his trade as a shipwright at Pembroke Dock when that great shipbuilding yard had been in its heyday, and he is said to have worked on the last boat to be built on Saundersfoot harbour in the 1860's-70's. He also had a boat of his own, but was not the most popular member of the harbour fraternity of that village, either amongst his fellow boatmen, or us village boys who sought their patronage and picked up much useful knowledge in the doing of it.

It is fair to say that his four daughters, who tended to keep their own company, and possibly because their contemporaries preferred it that way, were not exactly the best-loved ladies to be met with in the village. Be that as it may, in the spring of 1916, Bill Frost's younger son, Lawson, married Affie Bob's eldest daughter, Lizzie. He was in the army at the time, having been in the Territorial Army previously, and eventually saw service in India. When he returned he worked as an insurance agent, and he and Lizzie had one son, Alfred, who has already been mentioned as the inseparable mate of Jack Griffiths' son, Howard. Young Affie Frost would presumably have been named after his maternal grandfather, but inherited the musical talent of his father's father, and later in life played for years in a local dance band. To tell of some of their youthful capers would no doubt make for good reading and be highly diverting, but it is not for telling here.

There were perhaps one or two minor peccadilloes

which occurred in the succeeding years following Lawson's marriage, but when, in 1928, Affie Bob was caught stealing coal from a coal-truck on the harbour, if not exactly a *cause célèbre*, it was certainly the source of great hilarity and much ribald comment in the village.

The local *cognoscenti*, and that included the two pillars of the local gendarmerie, Sergeant Nicholas and P.C. Henton, knew full well that it had been going on for some time, but it could only be in reference to the incident in question that evidence could be given. The Sergeant's daughter, Crissy, was later to marry Bill Frost's young grandson, who was named after him, but the arresting officer was none other than the legendary P.C. Stanley Henton, who on one historic occasion had travelled in the company of the village football team to an away game and then had to turn out still wearing his policeman's uniform to keep goal when the Saundersfoot custodian failed to put in an appearance. Many a hilarious tale can be told of the fearless limb-of-the-law, Stan Henton. The defending solicitor appearing for Affie Bob was the equally legendary T. Bentley Mathias.

P.C. Henton told the Bench, when the case came before the court, that he had been travelling down St Bride's Hill in the car of young Mr Fred Hunt. I am not sure whether I should declare an interest at this point, because in later years I was to be Fred's best man when he married, and he also played in one of the dance bands of the day with Affie Frost, as well as accompanying me on the piano in the concert party days when I played the ukulele. On the occasion in question he was merely giving everybody's friend, Stan Henton, a lift, and the policeman was in civilian clothes. That did not prevent him from doing his duty when he spotted Affie Bob sitting in the hedge, taking a breather, but with a sack on his back. At sixty-eight years of age, suffering from rupture and having to wear a truss, he no doubt felt in need of it. He initially made the mistake of saying that he had hard coal in the bag which he had bought from Roger Griffiths, the village coalman and entrepreneur in general, but P.C. Henton knew that Roger Griffiths sold only soft coal and not hard coal. The bag was found to contain 71 lbs of coal which, at 45s per ton, was valued at 1s.8d. The colliery owner, C.H. Vickerman, was called to testify that it was his coal, and he was supported by the harbour master, Ambrose Lilbourne.

The scene of the confrontation had been on the bend at the bottom of St Bride's Hill, right opposite the beginning of Ragged Staff, within yards of the Bethany Manse, and I was thereabouts at the time, but, at nine years of age, was too young to be quoted, let alone called in evidence. Young Jack Ellis, however, was fifteen, and he was old enough to be called, and said that he worked for Mr William Beddoe, the butcher, and had seen defendant carrying the bag up from the harbour.

Under cross-examination Jack had to admit that his family were not exactly the best of friends with the Lewis family and, yes indeed, they could perhaps be described as enemies. Or, in Pembrokeshire parlance, they were not very 'greet'.

'The Moving Finger writes; and, having writ,
Moves on: nor all your Piety nor Wit
Shall lure it back to cancel half a Line,
Nor all your Tears wash out a Word of it.'

So, as Omar Khayam would have it to be, we are reminded by the recorded word that everything up St Bride's Lane was apparently not all sweetness and light, and the Ellises, a respected and well-liked family, lived alongside Bill Frost, father to Affie Bob's son-in-law, Lawson Frost, on the opposite side of the lane to Affie Bob, and the Frosts and Ellises were good friends and neighbours.

Affie Bob had pleaded not guilty, swore that he was home at the stated hour on the date in question, and his daughter, Sally, whose own daughter was subsequently to marry a gentleman of the Cloth, corroborated this. The Bench, however, did not believe either of them, found the case proved, and bound the defendant over in the sum of £5 to be of good behaviour. The newspaper report does not say for how long.

Rankling under the scandal of the case of the stolen coal, the Lewises hit back by reminding anybody who had forgotten, and just as though it were relevant, that Mrs Annie Frost, the gentlest and kindest of ladies, who lived next-door to her good friends, the Ellises, had had the misfortune to have a child out of wedlock when she was young. This was no doubt calculated, in accordance with most cases of scandal, to establish Affie Bob's daughters as being whiter than white, and one village wit was quoted as saying that if Saundersfoot's famous anthracite was good enough for Queen Victoria it could be good enough even for Alffie Bob's daughter.

Far worse than the shame of the coal was to come, however. Lawson Frost was one who had contributed much to the community as scoutmaster, with helping to run the very successful village football team, and in the life of the chapel, including being a local preacher. Then the blow fell. In the early 1930's he left his wife, Lizzy, the former Miss Lewis, and went off with another woman. Cissy Bob was next in line to Lizzy and never married, then came Sally, who married and had a daughter, Elva. Then came the youngest of the four girls, Louie, and that was the lady with whom Lawson now eloped. Some there were who might have said that he had jumped from the frying pan into the fire, but the popular line of village thinking at the time was that he must have been a glutton for punishment. Divorce, of course, would have been much more difficult, and sometimes impossible, to arrange in those days, so he just lived with her in that age when such a scandalous way of life was rather less fashionable than it is today.

These bare bones of the feud should be enough for it to be appreciated why the very name of Frost would have been pure poison to the Lewises, and why they would never have been a party to anything being said or published to the credit or glory of the world's first aviator.

In January, 1935, Mrs Annie Frost died. By that time Bill Frost was blind and unable to cope on his own, and his daughter, Ethel, had him up to care for him in her home at Penybanc, Ammanford. He took with him all the letters concerning his patent, but left behind only the copies of the plans and the specification referring to the patent itself.

During the short time Bill Frost was at Penybanc, Lawson, an outcast from his native heath, who had now established himself in the furniture business, first of all at Barry and subsequently at Southend-on-Sea, was able to come down to see his father, whereas he would never have dared to show his face up St Bride's Lane, and he borrowed the big envelope containing all the priceless letters to show to some people who had expressed an interest in them. Shortly afterwards, a mere seven weeks after the death of his beloved Annie, Bill Frost died.

His grand-daughter, Ethel's daughter Ena, who was a young woman of twenty-four at the time, recalled that the old man was a heavy smoker and almost to the end would call to Ethel to come and fill his pipe for him. He was, however, a life-long teetotaller, but not long before he died said he fancied a glass of beer, and he really enjoyed it.

During this brief period Stammers Cottage had been uninhabited, and Howard Griffiths recalled the tension in

100

his home on a Saturday morning a few days after Bill Frost died. His father's Uncle Isaac, Annie's brother, came to the house just before midday and asked where Jack, Howard's father, was. Mrs Griffiths said that he was at work but, since it was a Saturday, it was a half-day and he would be home shortly for his dinner. When Jack came home, Isaac asked him if he knew where the key for Stammers Cottage was. Isaac said he had been there, but there had been no sign of the key.

Before Bill Frost had married Annie, Stammers Cottage had been the Griffiths' family home since as far back as anybody could remember, their mother having been born there in 1821. There were family heirlooms, and some pieces of antique furniture, which were known to have been valuable even in those days. Time was to show that the Lewis family had the key and had cleared the cottage of everything. And everything included those few documents relating to his flying machine, which Bill Frost had not taken to Ammanford with him. Affie's widow, Olive, at the age of ninety, confirmed this, and said the story had been well-known throughout the years and handed down in the Frost family.

Sally's daughter, Elva, in later years married the local curate, Stanley Hobbs, who eventually became vicar of Amroth and Crunwear, before retiring to live in Saundersfoot, and he predeceased her. I once asked her about Bill Frost's documents, but she denied having any knowledge of them. She had, it transpired, given away what few odds and ends remained of Bill Frost's papers a few years before she died. The only letter included would appear to have been a copy of the one acknowledging the registration of his completed specification with the scale of charges in the event of renewal. She had given it to Lionel Allen, a near neighbour, whose house is built on the site of

Bill Frost's old cottage and workshop. He confirmed this when he spoke on the radio programme *Flying Starts* of Elva having told him that her family had obtained it when they cleared Bill Frost's cottage after he died.

Before that, in 1949, Lawson had died in Southend-on-Sea. His sister, Ethel, was by then too frail to travel up for the funeral, but her daughter, Ena, went. The envelope with the originals of the precious letters was there amongst his possessions, but Louie watched Ena's movements like a hawk. Ena's chances of having the letters returned to her, however, were finally scuppered by her refusal to take Lawson's budgerigars, Louie refusing to accept that their chances of survival would have been negligible in a house in Penybanc where there were three cats.

Parish pump, or small town, talk all of this may well be, but, if the world is interested and has ever wondered why such priceless letters could have been destroyed, the world now knows.

Chapter 11

Why The Sudden Interest?

There remains, then, the one question which has puzzled so many people of recent times. Why the sudden interest in a story which, it now has to be accepted, has been known in the area of Bill Frost's birthplace, where he lived and moved and had his being for all but a year or so of his long life, and yet has been ignored by the world for more than a hundred years?

In 1979, my novel, *Heronsmill*, set in this area, was published by Hutchinson, and shortly afterwards by St Martin's Press in America. In 1990 I had a letter from a complete stranger, Jeff Bellingham, of Minnesota, telling me that he had come across it by chance in his local library and found it very evocative. He said that his family had gone out to America from the Gloucester area, and that he remembered being taken on holiday to Saundersfoot by his parents when he was a small boy in the late 1930's. He said he had enjoyed the book so much that he had then ordered all the books I had written. Then, having made enquiries about the industrial history of the area, he had been sent a copy, by a gentleman by the name of Alec Thompstone, of my local history book, *Old Saundersfoot* (Gomer 1977), in which I had mentioned briefly the story of Bill Frost. His full story has now been told in far greater detail in these pages.

Without checking the historical facts on the dates of Orville Wright's flight, being content merely to quote the years given in the newspaper article of 1932, and therefore getting it slightly wrong, I had confined myself to referring to what I knew of Bill Frost personally, with a mere mention of what little I had ever been told of his flight. In the same book I told of many other things relating to the area in former days, most of which were known to those of my own generation, but unknown to so many of those who visit the area in the holiday season and those who have settled in the area, such as the helpful gentleman who had lived there for fifteen years and who gave me the fascinating information that the field where we had played as children was Beddoe's lake, which had been a big lake with boats on it fifty years ago. How fortunate I did not know about this when I wrote *Old Saundersfoot*, otherwise I might have made an even bigger fool of myself than nature had perhaps intended. But nobody questioned the veracity of anything I had written, including and especially the reference to Bill Frost's flight, and that was for the simple reason that Saundersfoot people had always known about it.

Whilst so much of what I wrote was of interest to natives, who were then delighted to reminisce, there was nothing new in it, including the reference to Bill Frost and his aeroplane. Inevitably people would then start asking me had I forgotten so-and-so, and whether I remembered such-and-such, and that included little snippets of information about Bill Frost, as well as about other happenings, which had either slipped my mind, or of which I had not heard.

It was one thing for Jeff Bellingham to have enjoyed *Heronsmill*, however, but something else entirely different for him to read about Bill Frost, because Jeff Bellingham was an engineer, an inventor, and a man with an interest in matters aeronautical.

When he wrote again he said he was coming to this country on a business visit and would like to meet me. If I could spare the time, he said, he would like to see something of the scenes where my books had been set, because that now included the new novel, *Crickdam*, which, along with another novel, *Roseanna* (Gomer 1991), was to complete the trilogy.

When Jeff eventually arrived, in June of the following year, and came to lunch, he surprised me greatly by producing a photostat copy of the original plan and specification which Bill Frost had lodged at the London Patent Office. Jeff had been in touch with them in the course of his business interest, had asked about the possibility of there being any record of Bill Frost's plans, and they had surprised him eventually by producing them. Perhaps it surprised me even more.

Later in the day I showed him the long-abandoned remains of the cottage at Heronsmill and the overgrown, choked-up leat to the mill itself. I showed him, too, the remains of the old ironworks at Stepaside, the site of the foundry, and the long-since abandoned iron ore workings at the patches at Crickdam. When I drove him back to Saundersfoot I showed him the field from which Bill Frost flew.

Jeff was staying at the Coppet Hall Hotel, Saundersfoot, which was being run at that time by a young couple whose parents, Rod and Ann Warwick, had moved in with them in partnership to help them, and Rod, Ann and Jeff formed an immediate rapport with each other.

Truth being stranger than fiction, just as if there have not already been more than enough carpenters to have moved through these pages, Rod Warwick, before his early retirement, had been a carpenter. Yes, another carpenter. And not just an ordinary carpenter.

At thirteen years of age he had started work at his native Winchester, learning his trade with Hutchinsons, a firm specialising in the manufacture of high quality hand-built caravans. When he was called up for National Service five years later he opted for the regular army. By the time he came back, twelve years later, the demand for high quality hand-built caravans had virtually disappeared, the only people who could afford them having been the old-established showground families and the genuine Romanys, who had also disappeared. So he went to work as a carpenter in the building trade. Eventually he did a ten-year stint with Formula 1, stripping and rebuilding racing cars.

Not surprisingly perhaps, he, too, was more than passing interested in the plans which Jeff now showed him. Having looked at them, he said, 'We could build this thing.' And that was when the seed was sown, and the idea took root to build a flying machine, working as faithfully as possible to Bill Frost's plans, and eventually fly it from the field from which Bill Frost made what might yet prove to have been a history-making flight.

By one of those odd quirks of fate, as a result of all that has happened to what was once known as Saundersfoot since the area suffered the blight cast upon it once it had been designated a National Park, of the ten percent which has not yet been built on, the field at Griffithston Hill remains.

One thought contributed by Rod as they discussed the technicalities of the design together was the probability that Bill Frost would have used bamboo in the making of a machine to such a design. And that was before he had any idea that Frost had been quoted long ago as having said that he had indeed used bamboo.

106

Jeff returned to Minnesota and began to work on his plans. Meanwhile he sent Rod a copy of Bill Frost's drawing and the brief specification, and Rod was sufficiently interested and impressed by the apparently unvarnished truth and credibility of the story, with its infinite possibilities, that he framed the copy of plan and specification and put them up on the wall for the benefit of those paying guests who might be interested in what most of them would no doubt regard as such an unlikely story.

One such inquisitive, interested and highly amused sceptic to turn up quite by chance to stay at the Coppet Hall Hotel in the early summer of 1993 was a friend of mine, the well-known journalist, Byron Rogers. Having seen the framed documents on the wall, he telephoned me, and I convinced him sufficiently of the authenticity of the story for him to decide to look into it more fully and do a story on it for the *Sunday Telegraph,* for which paper at that time he was contributing a highly popular column under the title *Village Voice.*

In due course, the appointment was made, Byron came down from his exile in England, and I took him to Saundersfoot. He talked to Frankie Williams, who was ninety-one years old at the time, and he talked to Charlie Cox, another genuine 'Old Sandersfooter' no longer with us, but at that time in his eighties, who had been born and brought up within a hundred yards of Bill Frost. Byron talked also to the more technically-minded Paul Williams, and the more he heard the more he became convinced that the story of Bill Frost and his aeroplane was perhaps not after all some sort of romantic nonsense that had recently been dreamed up as a publicity stunt or advertising gimmick for the popular holiday area.

Then he went back to his exile in England and wrote up his story. The *Sunday Telegraph,* possibly being more

107

interested at that time in those new-found country types with three acres and a hen, declined to use a story which seemed to them to be so much nonsense. So Byron sold the story to the *Guardian*, and it appeared in their weekend edition of July 17th, 1993.

From there on the interest grew, with other newspapers doing follow-up stories, and with various interviews on radio and television. One was a particularly interesting programme, called *Flying Starts*, on BBC Radio 4 on August 1st, 1998. It transpired that the producer, Jill Waters, had seen Byron's feature in the *Guardian* when she was on the staff of the BBC, and had made a note of it as one of the programmes she would like to do one day when she eventually became a freelance. The presenter was Patrick French, a relative of the immortal Percy French of Irish and world fame. They, too, cast their net a little wider and spoke to Bill Frost's great-great-grand-daughter, Nina Ormonde, and her eleven-year-old daughter, Jessica, at school in Saundersfoot. The same stories had come down to them in one form or another over the years, the same as they have come down to so many in the area, even where there is inevitably a variation in detail, and lack of any sort of proof to substantiate different statements. Few there are left now who can speak with any real authority.

The *Sunday Times*, as it happened, had picked up the story from an advance press notice, and did a story on July 26th ahead of the broadcast. So the momentum grew, and suddenly the world seemed to be asking who was this Bill Frost and what flying machine was that then?

Chapter 12

After Jeff Bellingham

Disappointing though it was, after the great enthusiasm on the other side of the Atlantic, matters were not destined to develop as had been planned. *Nam homo proponit, sed Deus disponit* wrote Thomas À Kempis, a good many years before either Bill Frost or Jeff Bellingham came on the scene, which is to say, 'Man proposes, but God disposes.'

At least one good thing to come out of it was the fact that my wife and I were to form a very happy personal friendship with Jeff. Sadly, however, when his plans were well advanced, but when there was still much to be done by way of raising the necessary finances for such a project, Jeff's wife became ill, and died after a long illness. Only those of us who have walked that dark and lonely road know what it can do to us. It would be no more than mere hyperbole to point out, as those who have also walked the same road know only too well, that not surprisingly, at that point, Jeff effectively ended his practical association with any ideas on a huge project to finance single-handed the building and flying of a replica of Bill Frost's flying machine, and indeed, shortly after his wife's death, he sold his engineering business.

In the meantime Byron Rogers had appeared on the

scene. Normally, it is the proper function of journalists to write about the news, not to make it, unless they happen to do something nefarious or irresponsible, and are asked by a uniformed officer of the law please to blow into this, sir. But make the news, or at least cause the news to be created, most certainly Byron did. Following his visit to the Coppet Hall Hotel, and his initial article in the *Guardian*, the telephone bell began to ring.

Of the many newspaper features, radio and television programmes, perhaps the most interesting initially was the very good 1998 radio programme *Flying Starts*, already referred to, and the interest engendered by the story in advance of it in the *Sunday Times*. It was something of a story, too. Not merely that this previously unheralded and unsung village carpenter in the backwoods of the far west of Wales had built and flown his machine all those years ago, but that somebody was coming over from America, above all places, to prove that it had been done before the Wright brothers of America's own Kitty Hawk fame. Yes, it certainly looked as if history might be about to be rewritten.

Of those sufficiently enthusiastic to carry on where, by this time, Jeff Bellingham had left off, was a small independent Cardiff-based television company, Raw Charm. They had obtained sufficient evidence from the research of others, particularly myself, to convince the technical people at the Qinetic Aerospace Research and Development Centre, at RAF Boscombe Down in Wiltshire, that the project was worth consideration. And so, if it meant having to rewrite history, then history would have to be rewritten, and so what, because history is having to be rewritten all the time?

According to a Pamela Hunt of Raw Charm, writing in the magazine, *Pembrokeshire Life*, in January 2007, the work at Boscombe Down came to a premature halt when Britain

110

and the USA invaded Iraq. The same writer also tells us that, before the characters at Boscombe Down had to draw their research to an end, they had come to the conclusion that Bill Frost could not have flown his 'plane.

So where do we now have to look to find out whereabouts in what backwoods somebody or other flew even before Bill Frost? There has never been any argument or doubt whatsoever amongst those who knew, as to whether Bill Frost did fly, whether the scientists can prove it or not, even though highly qualified aeronautical engineers, including such as they may or may not have at Boscombe Down, have proved conclusively that a bumble bee, with its inadequate wings in relation to the size and weight of its body, could not possibly fly.

Be that as it may, perhaps Bill Frost did not know much about bumble bees and their limitations, which would be why he, too, managed to fly. And fly he most certainly did.

Patent Drawing

A.D. 1894. Oct. 25. N: 20,431.

FROST'S Complete Specification.

(1 SHEET)

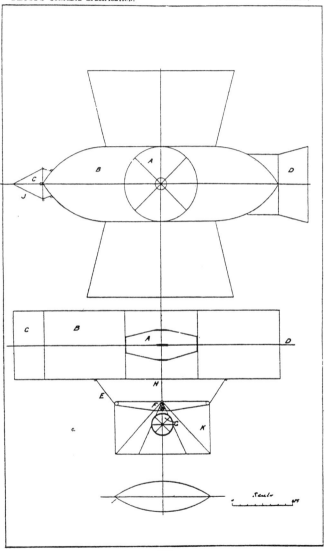

INDEX

A

Aerial Steam Transit Company 22
Aeronautical Society of Great
   Britain 22
Air-Britain Digest 15
Airships 47
Allen, Charles Smith 16
   "   H. Mortimer 16
   "   Lionel 101
   "   Samuel J. 16
Amroth 28, 36, 101
Apolyn of Trinovantum 20

B

Badham, Doris (née Watkins) 47
   "   John 47
   "   Will 47
Bamboo 74, 106
Beddoe, Frank 65
   "   William (Billy) 48, 65, 98
Beddoe's Lake 78,
Beddoe's Yard 77, 78
Bellingham, Jeff 103-107, 109
Besnier's flying apparatus 21
Bethany Manse 31, 39, 47, 98
Bishop Wilkins 21
Bladud, king of Bath 20
Bonville's Court pit, 25, 27, 35-37
Borelli 22
Boscombe Down 110, 111
Broadfield Cottage 38
bumble bees 44, 110

C

Cale, Thomas 92, 93
Canvas 37, 74, 81
Cayley, Sir George 22
Census Returns 25-29, 38
Chapels: Bethany 30-32, 46, 67
   "   Bethesda 27, 43, 48, 67
   "   St. Andrew's Calvanistic
      Methodist 27, 93
Clift Cottage 26
Complete Specification 14
Coppet Hall Hotel 105, 107, 110

Cox, Charlie 107
Crickdam 8
Crickdam [Gomer 1990] 36, 37, 105

D

Daedalus 19
Davies, Billy 45
   "   Jeremiah 27
   "   Mel 67
   "   Rebecca 29

E

Ellis, Jack 98

F

F.A. Cup Final 78, 79
Fishguard invasion 25
Flying Starts 102, 108, 110
Formula 1 racing cars 106
Foxenholes 48
French, Patrick 108
From Amroth to Utah 28
Frost, Alfred 45, 96, 97
   "   Annie 44, 99, 100
   "   Bill, son of John &
      Rebecca 11, 26
   "   Edith 28,
   "   Ethel 28, 29, 47, 66, 92,
      100, 102
   "   John ...Chartist leader 24
   "   John, related to Chartist
      leader 25-27
   "   Lawson 29, 92, 93, 96-100,
      102
   "   Margaretta (née Thomas)
      28, 29, 34, 38, 44, 67
   "   Mary...wife of John 25
   "   Olive 100, 101
   "   Rebecca 25-27
   "   Sarah dtr. of John &
      Rebecca 26-29,38
   "   Wilfred 28, 29, 40, 45-48,
      65, 78
   "   William son of John &
      Rebecca 24, 26

113

"   "   (Billy) 48
"   William…father of John 24
G
Geoffrey of Monmouth 20
Goldschmit, Otto 88
Griffiths, Annie 29, 68, 93
"   Howard 45, 96, 100
"   Isaac 29, 93, 101
"   Jack 29, 44, 46, 65, 101
"   Jim 29
"   John 29
"   Mark 29
"   Roger 98
Griffithston, 25, 26, 38
"   Cottage 38, 39
"   Hill 11, 27, 29, 38-40,
             47, 48, 77, 106
"   Lane 39, 78
Grove 35, 36
Guardiani 108, 110
H
Hean Castle, 35, 37, 70, 77
Henson 22
Henton P.C., Stanley 97, 98
Heronsmill 103-105
Hilling, Billy 48
"   Hettie 67
"   Lewis 48, 67
Hobbs, Elva 99-102
"   Stanley 101
Hopshill 26
Howell, Ivor 39
'Hungry Nineties' 30, 89
Hunt, Fred 97
"   Pamela 110
Hutchinsons, caravan
    builders 106
I
Icarus, The Quest Of -19
Illustrated Official Journal
    (Patents) No: 527 85, 90
Industrial Saundersfoot
    [M.R.C.Price] 36
iron foundry 36, 105

iron ore 36, 105
ironworks 36, 37, 105
J
Jalna Hotel 31
Jones, Francis-Wales Herald
    Extraordinary 35
K
Kitty Hawk 23, 110
L
Labyrinth of Crete 19
Lack, H. Reader, *Comptroller-
    General of Patents* 85, 90
Lady of the Isles 45
Landsker 76
Leonardo da Vinci 21
Lewis, Alfred Henry,
          ('Affie Bob') 95-99
"   Cissy 99
"   Lizzie 96, 99
"   Louie 99, 102
"   Sally 99, 101
Lilbourne, Ambrose 98
Lind, Jenny 74, 88
Little England Beyond Wales 33
London 92, 93
Long Park 77
Lord Merthyr 70
Lord Milford 36
Lower Level pit 35
M
Marquis of Bacqueville 21
Mathias, T. Bentley 97
Maxim, Sir Hiras 23
Merlewood 31
Milton 20
Minnesota 103, 107
Minos 19
Mortimer, Ena 47, 93, 100, 102
Moy, Thomas 22
N
Narberth Weekly News 32, 42, 46,
    68
Nash, Bobby 48, 65
"   Lewis 25

114

" Mary 25
" Rebecca 25, 48
Nicholas Sgt., Mathias 97
" Crissy 97

O

Old Saundersfoot [Gomer 1977] 36, 103, 104
Oliver of Malemsbury 20
Ormonde, Jessica 108
" Nina 108

P

Patent Office, London 69, 87, 105
Paucton 22
Pembroke Dock 70, 73, 77, 93, 96
Pembrokeshire Herald and General Advertiser 12
Pembrokeshire Life 110
Penybanc, Ammanford 47, 66, 93, 100, 101
Philipps, Picton Castle Estate 35, 36
Plantation Cottages 30, 45
Pont Royal 21
Professor Langley 23
Prout, Mary 28
Provisional Specification 12, 89

Q

Qinetic Aerospace Research 110
Queen Victoria 35, 82, 99

R

Railway Street 27, 28, 35, 38
Rhodewood 39
Raw Charm 110
Ragged Staff 39, 98
railway line 36
Recorded Patents void…92
Richards, Fred 45
Roblin's Corner 45
Roblin, Tom 45
Rogers, Byron 107-110
Rosalind 28
Roseanna [Gomer 1991] 105
Royal Letters Patent 83
Royal Seal 15

Royal Yacht 35

S

sailing ships 35, 37
Sandy Hill 39, 45
Santos-Dumont, M. Alberte 71
Saundersfoot, anthracite 35
" beach 65
" harbour 35-37, 45, 96
" High Street 45
" Male Voice Choir 32, 33
St Bride's Hill 31, 39, 97, 98
St Bride's Lane 29, 30, 39, 65, 67, 93, 95, 98, 100
St Issell's 27, 67
Stammers Cottage 30, 45, 68, 93, 95, 100, 101
Stammers Mountain 39
Stammers Road 39, 40
Tennyson House 95
The Strand 27
three tunnels 36, 40
tramroad 40
Science Museum 22
Seine 21
sheet metal 37
Sload 18
Southend-on-Sea 100, 102
St Edmund's Church, Harfield, Bristol 24
St John Brodrick, Under-Secretary of State 72, 88
Steart 18, 48, 79, 81
Stepaside 28, 36, 105
Stokes, Thomas 37
Stringfellow and Wenham 22
Sunday Telegraph 107
Sunday Times 108, 110
Sunderland flying-boats 77

T

Taylor, David 48
Tenby and County News 12, 15
Tenby Observer 32, 65, 68

Tenby, Bridge Street 25
"   great gale 16
"   harbour 16, 17
"   lifeboat 16
"   pier 16
"   South beach 77
"   St Andrew's private
      school 40
"   St Julian Street 25
The People 73-76, 87, 88
Thomas À Kempis 109
Thomas, James 27, 32
"   Margaretta 27, 34
Thompstone, Alec 103
*Treasury Of Historic
   Pembrokeshire* 35
Tuileries 21
Twycross 40
V
Vickerman, C.H. 98
"   Charles Ranken 35-37
"   John 36
Village Voice 107

W
Walters, H.G. (Glyn) 68, 76, 77
Warwick, Ann 105
"   Rod 105, 107
Waters, Jill 108
Watkins, Doris 47
"   Fred 47
"   Josie 39, 47
"   Sarah 29, 38, 47
"   William 29, 38
Weddle, Billy 78
Well Field 18
Western Mail 68, 76, 87
White House 45
Williams, George 46
"   Frankie 46, 107
"   Paul 15, 87, 88, 107
Winchester 106
Wisemansbridge 36, 40
Wogan Street 26

Woodside, brickworks 36
Wright, Wilbur and Orville 23,
   47, 71, 104, 110

A RURAL MISCELLANY
by Roscoe Howells; £6.90
Gwasg Carreg Gwalch

Rural areas and their communities have seen many changes over the past half century. No one has been closer to those people, lands and changes than Roscoe Howells – a former farmer and agricultural journalist.

For twelve years, his weekly 'Ben Brock' column in the *Welsh Farm News* was the highlight of the week for many of its readers, who knew that a laugh would never be far away. A widely-published author, and an authority on the history of the Pembrokeshire islands and the area in which he lives, Roscoe Howells became the first Welsh member of the Guild of Agricultural Journalists and the first to appear in the Fisons Annual Awards.

Provocative, prophetic and at times unashamedly passionate, this collection of articles penned by Roscoe Howells is rewarding in so many ways.

I would like to order .... copy/copies of 'A Rural Miscellany' at £6.90 each adding £1.50 for postage.
Payment by cheque payable to Gwasg Carreg Gwalch, or phone 01492 642031 with card details.

Name ....

Address ....

....

....

Tel: ....

A Rural Miscellany

Roscoe Howells

If you have enjoyed reading this book and been tantalised in Chapter 11 by references to **Heronsmill**, set in the Saundersfoot area, this well-loved and timeless title has been reprinted by Emissary and is available from all good bookshops or direct from Emissary Publishing, PO Box 33, Bicester, OX26 4ZZ, at £8.50 plus £1.00 p&p. in UK.

HERONSMILL (318 pages) by Roscoe Howells

'It's a fortnight's solid read in a harvest field with your feet up listening to larks ... this tale of country folk, their loves and hates, their customs, is like a prescription for our troubled age. For those who seek this peace, it is all here – the people, the sky, the good earth.'

Alexander Cordell

In the face of the worst that fate can do, and the loss of an old way of life, Eben Harter struggles to hold on to all the values which were ingrained in him during an age gone beyond recall. Filled, as a boy, with the wonder of growing things, he reaches manhood with all the kindliness and integrity that life at remote **Heronsmill** has given him. But progress and two world wars bring inevitable changes to the simplicity of a country way of life, not least to the farming in which he eventually becomes heavily committed. They bring changes to Eben Harter and his family, too.